W9-BBQ-083

DISCARDED

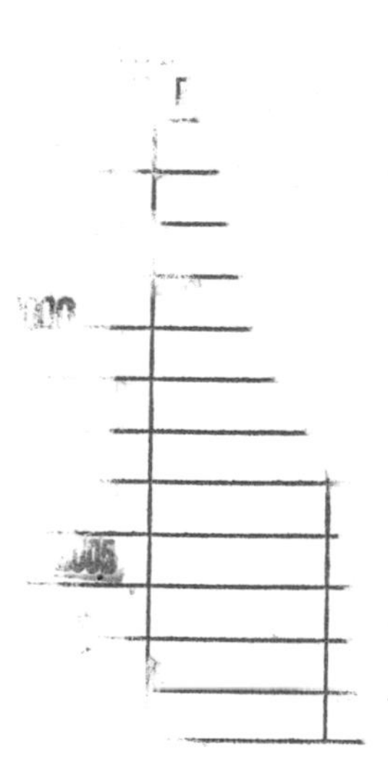

Better Homes and Gardens®

# *Your Child* LIVING WITH DIVORCE


First Edition. First Printing.
Library of Congress Catalog Card Number: 89-63157
ISBN: 0-696-01885-3

**YOUR CHILD: LIVING WITH DIVORCE**
Editor: Elizabeth Woolever
Contributing Editor: Mary Conroy
Editorial Project Manager: Angela K. Renkoski
Graphic Designer: Mary Schlueter Bendgen
Electronic Text Processor: Paula Forest
Contributing Photographers: Kathryn Abbe, Jim Kascoutas
Contributing Illustrator: Clint Hansen

**ACKNOWLEDGMENTS**
Colette Davison, Child and Family Psychotherapist, Chicago.
Dr. Emily Visher, Psychologist, and Dr. John Visher, Psychiatrist; Co-founders of the Stepfamily Association of America, Lafayette, California.
Judi Lodden, M.A., Family Therapist, West Des Moines, Iowa.
Florence Kaslow, Ph.D., Director, Florida Couples and Family Institute, West Palm Beach, Florida.
Roger Burt, Ph.D., Step By Step Counseling Center, Baltimore, Maryland.

Divorce is never easy, even if everyone involved has decided it's for the best. Dealing with your child's reactions while you're still in pain can be exhausting. Starting over takes hard work, but your family will be stronger for your efforts. This book gives you helpful information to guide you through the process, from the initial stages to preparing to remarry and build a stepfamily.

# TALKING WITH CHILDREN

Good relationships with kids are based on communication. During and after a divorce, this is even more important: Your children will feel they can trust you if you've been honest, no matter how painful it is initially. You can best reassure them by opening the lines of communication before divorce and then keeping them open.

Open communication doesn't happen overnight. It takes daily effort and a willingness to express and hear ideas and feelings you might want to avoid. But the rewards of a healthier, happier family are well worth the work.

## Discussing the Divorce

Long before you tell your children about the divorce, they'll sense tension in the house. If you pretend that everything is just fine, they'll begin to lose faith in you. It's better to acknowledge their feelings and stress that you still love them. You might say, "Daddy and I aren't getting along very well, but we still love you." That won't erase all their fears—after all, they should worry about a divorce. But it will tell them that you are committed to them.

You shouldn't involve the children in a debate over separation, however. Instead, keep your thoughts to yourself until you've definitely decided to separate. Discussing divorce is hard enough without adding the "maybe-we-will, maybe-we-won't" element.

Once you've decided, the discussion should follow soon after. Explaining divorce is never easy. You may wonder if toddlers need an explanation, or if it will confuse them. You may worry that you'll scare your children if you cry during the discussion.

Despite your reservations, a family meeting is essential. A fair, compassionate discussion can help kids weather the storm with grace. Many experts say that a child's adjustment depends largely on a good, honest explanation.

Whenever possible, both parents should tell the children together. A joint discussion reassures kids that you both still love them and plan to stay involved in their lives. When both of you talk to them, they realize that you will continue to make decisions about them together and that they can depend on both of you. It also helps kids to avoid thinking that the divorce is only one person's idea, or that one parent is to blame.

Of course, in some situations, such as abandonment, one person really is to blame. If that's the case, the other parent can explain the divorce in a matter-of-fact manner. Also, if one parent refuses to participate, the other should take the initiative. It's better for kids to hear from only one parent than to be left in the dark.

Even the most careful explanation will be understood differently by each child. Age, personality, previous losses, and family relationships all influence a child's comprehension. You may want to explain divorce in separate sessions for older and younger children. Some couples bring all the kids together, but talk to each one individually in front of the others. This way the children can comfort one another, but still get the information they need at a level they can understand.

But no matter how you decide to tell them, include the following information:

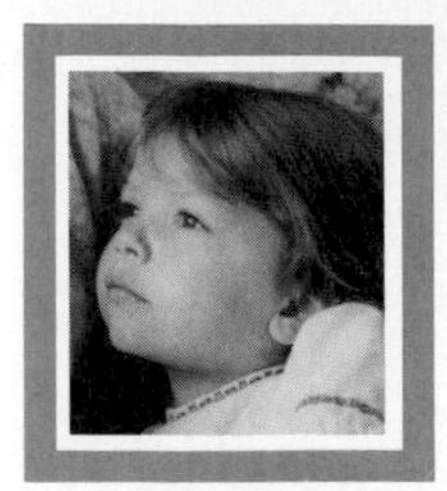



- why you are divorcing;
- what changes the children can expect;
- that they can rely on continued love and support from both of you.

You don't need a catalog of marital problems to explain the reasons for divorce. But you do need some reason, because children who do not hear a reason will draw their own conclusions. Often, they will blame themselves and continue to feel guilty for years for "causing" the divorce. Even as simple an explanation as "We don't get along anymore" will help prevent children from blaming themselves. State clearly that it is not the children's fault, that it is a problem between the two of you.

After you've told them why you're divorcing, older children, with their greater understanding of and curiosity about relationships, may have more detailed questions than younger ones. They may query you closely about affairs, arguments, or substance abuse. Although it's important to be honest with them, you don't have to tell them things that you consider private. They may test you, but if you have been honest with them, your children eventually will accept your need for privacy. You can express that need by saying, "I've given you all the answers I feel you need to know. The rest is private."

Telling the children how their lives will be different is important because some children have no idea what divorce means; others imagine the worst. All kids like to know what changes the divorce will bring, instead of trying to imagine the new life themselves. Let them know what to expect by explaining who will live where, how they can get access to the noncustodial parent, and when they can visit the noncustodial parent.

Be aware that no matter how gently you explain divorce, most children will feel afraid and abandoned. Their world is crumbling, and they may conclude that the noncustodial parent no longer wants them. To ease their fears, tell them that you both will still love them and be there for them.

Because divorce arouses such fears, your children may be too anxious at first to hear your explanation. Be prepared to answer their questions over and over again. It may seem exasperating, but children find reassurance in the mere fact that your answers don't change. Each time you answer their questions, they will find the separation a little easier to tolerate.

## Working Together As Parents

Explaining divorce with your ex-spouse signals a united front to the kids. But long after the divorce, your relationship with your ex-spouse will influence the kids. Your children will have fewer problems if you and your ex-spouse cooperate.

Cooperating may be difficult if you still have strong feelings about the divorce and your ex-spouse. But cooperation doesn't mean pretending to love your ex-spouse for the children's sake. It simply means conveying to the kids that your ex-spouse is still their parent and deserves respect. It will help if you separate yourself emotionally from your ex-spouse by keeping your children's best interests in mind.

Most problems that emerge for children of divorce result from one parent undermining the other. Some parents use kids as go-betweens, sabotage the other parent's attempts to stay close to the kids, or criticize the other parent in front of the children. You may feel justified in undermining your ex-spouse, particularly if you disapprove of that parent's lifestyle. You may also feel vindicated in undermining if you didn't initiate the divorce or didn't agree with it. But when kids hear you criticize their other parent, they feel the sting as deeply as if you'd criticized them. Many parents hope that the children will side with them, but the strategy backfires: Kids only come to resent the parent who undermines the other.

Try to avoid putting the kids between the two of you. Don't ask a child to carry messages to your ex-spouse or to report on your ex-spouse's new life. It puts the child in a bad position and breeds resentment.

## How to Tell the Children

How much children understand depends a great deal on the age of the child. The explanation you give an adolescent might bewilder a younger child, and an adolescent would be insulted by the explanation you give your toddler. A few sample explanations for children of different age groups follow.

**For children younger than 7:**
***Mother:*** "Your daddy and I have been fighting too much, so we are going to get a divorce."
***Father:*** "We won't be married anymore. I'll live in another house, and you'll stay there on weekends. I'll visit you here, too. We feel very sad, but this is the best thing to do."
***Mother:*** "We used to love each other, but now we don't. We won't be married, but we'll always be your mom and dad."
***Father:*** "We will still always love you, and we will never leave you alone."

**For children from 7 to 12:**
***Father:*** "You've noticed that your mom and I aren't getting along. We've talked about our problems, but we haven't solved them, and we only make each other unhappy. We have decided to get divorced. It makes us sad, but it's the best decision for everyone."
***Mother:*** "We won't be married to each other anymore, and we will live in separate houses. You will live with Daddy, and I will live in an apartment a few miles away. But you can call me anytime you want to or ride your bike over to visit. And you will stay with me on weekends and all summer long."
***Father:*** "Sometimes children worry that a divorce is their fault and that their parents won't want to see them again. But it's not your fault. Your mother and I used to love each other, but over the years we just became too different to live together. This is a grown-up decision to divorce, but it doesn't change our feelings for you. We are still your parents, and we will still take care of you."
***Mother:*** "We may not love each other, but we both have a special love for you. And we always will."

**For adolescents:**
***Mother:*** "You've probably noticed that your dad and I don't get along very well. When we first got married, we loved each other very much. But sometimes adults' feelings change over time, and that's what happened here."
***Father:*** "Your mother and I just don't love each other anymore. We have decided that it would be better for everyone if we got a divorce. I'm moving out to an apartment in New York. The judge will ask whether you'd like to live with your mother or with me, and then you will go to live wherever the judge thinks is best. It might turn out that you will live with your mom during the school year and stay with me during vacation. But no matter where you live, we'll call you often, and you can call us anytime."
***Mother:*** "Just because Dad and I have grown apart, it doesn't mean we want to be apart from you. We feel sad that we can't live together anymore, but that doesn't change the way we feel about you."
***Father:*** "We tried hard, but we haven't been able to solve our problems. And the longer we stay together, the more unhappy we get. It's nobody's fault; we just changed. And you couldn't have prevented the divorce. But we both will always love you, and we will always be there for you whenever you need us."

When you need to contact your ex-spouse, do so by calling or talking in person. Don't expect a child to mediate where adults' efforts have failed.

Some children assume you need them to mediate, even though you've never said so. If you and your ex-spouse have heated arguments in front of the kids, one of them may step in to "protect" you. They also may misbehave after a phone call from your ex-spouse if the two of you are fighting.

In those cases, it helps to establish some ground rules. Discuss the situation with your ex-spouse, explaining the effect of the arguments on the children. Then come to some agreement so that you two can solve problems without worrying the children.

For instance, you might agree to call one another only after the kids are in bed; at all other times, the parents will call only to talk with the kids. Or you might decide to meet in person, without the children, to resolve issues. Either approach should help each of you separate your role as parent from your role as ex-spouse.

## Responsive Listening

Parents cope with the aftermath of divorce in different ways. Some have little energy left over for their kids, and the children can feel ignored. Others go to the opposite extreme and devote all their energy to the children, trying to solve every problem for them. Their kids can feel smothered.

But children don't have to feel neglected or squelched. If they know you are listening, they feel secure that you still love them. Listening can be even more helpful than solving their problems. Kids who feel someone is listening often get enough relief to solve their own problems. One way to empathize with them is by using the technique called responsive listening.

When you use responsive listening, you paraphrase both the content and emotions in a child's message. This gives your child the chance to feel understood or to correct the message if it was misinterpreted. To show that you understand the content, rephrase the facts; to show empathy, rephrase the feelings. Kids get annoyed if you merely repeat the message, so avoid quoting your child word for word.

Suppose your child says, "Mom gave me a doll even though I told her I wanted make-up. She knows I'm too old for dolls!" To paraphrase the content, you might answer: "She remembered your birthday present, but it wasn't quite what you wanted, right?"

To paraphrase the feelings, you might say, "It bothers you when people don't notice how grown up you are."

In that case, your child was just looking for a sympathetic ear, not asking for help. But at other times, your child may discuss a problem, tempting you to offer a solution. Even in these situations, you can use responsive listening to empathize but allow your child some independence.

For instance, your teenage daughter may say, "Dad got tickets for the ball game Saturday. It's my first night game, and he wants me to sleep over. But David asked me out for Sunday breakfast."

Your response might be: "A night game? Sounds exciting! I can see why you're torn between sleeping over and Sunday breakfast."

The first sentence shows that you got the facts; the next two show that you understand your daughter's dilemma. By answering in this way, you demonstrate that those feelings are important and natural, but you are letting your child make the decision.

Children do not always express their feelings directly, even when the feelings are ready to bubble over. By noticing their facial expressions and gestures, you can pick up on those unspoken feelings. If your son says about his stepmother, "Sue scolded me in front of everyone," and blushes, you might say, "Sounds embarrassing!"

Observing gestures and facial expressions also helps when your child says one thing but really means another. Usually, the nonverbal expressions are a more accurate indicator of your child's feelings.

For instance, your son might say, "So Dad's moving. Big deal. Doesn't matter to me. He's got a right to live where he wants. And I'm old enough to take care of myself."

Meanwhile, you notice your son's clenched fists. By saying, "You're pretty angry at him, aren't you?" you give him permission to talk about feelings he may have considered bad. You also give him the chance to correct you in case you've misinterpreted his feelings. He may say, "Maybe a little angry. But I'm more hurt than anything else."

## Open-Ended Questions

Some children find it hard to share their feelings. Others try to protect parents by burying their hurt or anger and pretending that everything is all right. Still, most children are relieved when they can talk openly about their concerns.

Open-ended questions encourage children to express their own ideas and emotions. These questions have no right or wrong answers, so they allow for a wide range of opinions. Open-ended questions may begin with "how" or "what." A few examples:

"How do you feel about moving?"

"What do you think about spending the summer with your mother?"

"Tell me about your new classroom."

Some children feel there's a taboo against expressing certain feelings, such as resentment. You can encourage children by mentioning your own feelings before you ask an open-ended question. For instance: "I was so sad when we had to leave that nice big house and move here. I really miss our old neighbors. How do you feel?"

## Special Situations

Attempting to hide such problems as infidelity, violence, homosexuality, and substance abuse is both futile and harmful. Often, the children suspect something is wrong; denying problems or hiding them only creates distrust.

It's important to be appropriately honest with children, but your life needn't be an open book. "Appropriately" is the key word; children only have to be told the general facts they can comprehend. A blow-by-blow account of an extramarital affair would overwhelm any child; instead, it's enough to explain, "Mommy doesn't love Daddy any-more. She loves someone else." If your child asks for details, you have every right to say, "Some issues are private."

If your spouse is a substance abuser or is mentally ill, your child probably senses that. When you explain the divorce, acknowledge the problem and express sympathy for your spouse. For instance, you might say, "Your father drinks too much and that's what makes him so angry. I feel very sad for him, but I can't live with him anymore."

Explaining abandonment is another matter. Telling a child, "Your mother loves you even though she never calls," simply isn't honest; love requires communication. It's better to be honest than to use euphemisms. If the other parent has abandoned the family and will have nothing to do with any of you, don't try to pretend that the communication will return some day. That pretense will only lead the children to hang on to hope unrealistically. In the end, they'll be disappointed and wonder why you led them on.

If your ex-spouse has abandoned them, tell your children something similar to, "Daddy doesn't want to be with us now. I don't know why he left, but he must be in pain to leave like that. But it wasn't anything you did. He didn't leave because of you." That will teach the kids compassion and spare them the anguish of wondering what they did to make that parent leave.

Extra support is a real comfort in these special cases. Self-help groups and readings can let you know that you're not alone. A therapist can be another source of emotional support in troubled times.

# GENERAL REACTIONS

## Tumultuous but Typical Reactions

Divorce produces many conflicting emotions for adults and children. For parents struggling with their own feelings, it's often hard to deal with their kids' reactions, too. But it's easier to comfort your children if you know what kinds of responses you can expect. It's also easier if you remember that all these feelings are natural and need to be expressed, no matter what your child's age or situation.

## Shock

Any major life change—a move, the birth of a sibling—may upset children. Divorce is no different. Some children are especially shocked by divorce if their parents never fought in front of them. But even in the angriest of families, where the children have pleaded with their parents to get a divorce, the announcement of divorce may throw children off balance. They are shocked because they have never imagined life without the two parents. "I never thought it would happen to our family" is an all-too-familiar refrain.

Older children are more likely to voice their shock because they have the vocabulary to do so. Younger children may not express their surprise in words, but may act it out. Other children will go numb, as if they've had an actual physical shock. They may appear to have little reaction to your divorce, or they may seem to be coping quite well because they never burst into tears or have tantrums. In most cases, that initial calm is deceiving; it usually masks feelings that are simply too painful for them to experience at that time.

Because the children will be stunned by your announcement, they literally may not hear what you are saying. They may ask you to repeat an explanation that was difficult enough the first time around. But patience in the face of your children's questions pays off. Every time you re-explain the divorce, telling the same story, your children will feel a bit more secure.

Besides explaining the divorce again and again, you can help your children cope with shock by gently prodding them to express their feelings. Open-ended questions can help them deal with feelings they'd rather ignore. Such questions let them know that it's OK to have these scary feelings and that talking about them relieves pressure.

## Denial

Shock often leads to another typical reaction: denial. It's perfectly normal for children to go through a period of pretending that the marriage is still intact. Some children ask no questions about the divorce. They put the divorce out of their minds and try to pretend that life will go on just the way it did before. They might not tell their friends about the divorce, thinking that the divorce isn't real as long as they don't tell anyone.

Denial allows children to temporarily escape the painful feelings they eventually must face. It also lets them avoid the

thought that they caused the divorce. Although denial is typical at first, continued denial long after the divorce is a sign that a child needs professional help.

Even if they don't deny the divorce, most children have reunification fantasies, and they may daydream that their parents will reconcile and remarry. Often children work to make that dream come true. "If I'm good, then Mom and Dad will get back together again" is a common, though usually unspoken, idea. Extremely good, helpful behavior may indicate that your child is hoping for a reconciliation.

Other children take the opposite approach and develop behavior problems or even physical illnesses to reunite their parents. Without realizing it, these children may assume, "If I have problems, Mom and Dad will have to get back together to help me."

Many children act out denial during play. When they play with dolls, some children insist on putting a mother and a father doll into bed together over and over again. Others endlessly draw pictures of a happy family that includes both parents. Don't intrude on your child's play because that may be a way of venting feelings.

In any of these cases, take the time to re-explain that the divorce is final. The burden of putting parents back together is far too great for any child to assume.

Sometimes the children are reflecting a parent's denial. When one parent resists the divorce, that message may be conveyed to the children in subtle ways. If either you or your ex-spouse have your own reunification fantasies, you won't be able to dispel your child's fantasies. A marital therapist can help you sort out your feelings about divorce so that you can put the fantasies to rest and get on with your life.

## Embarrassment

Closely related to the problem of denial is embarrassment or shame. The good news about embarrassment is that today's high divorce rates have reduced somewhat the embarrassment some children feel because more children come from divorced homes. The bad news is that children who feel embarrassed usually don't tell anyone they feel that way. It's hard enough to feel embarrassed without letting the whole world know why they think they deserve to feel that way.

Many youngsters feel ashamed because they want to be like their friends more than

### It's Over

Unless you explain that the divorce is final, the children may continue to try to reunite you and your ex-spouse. A frank discussion will allow them to put their energy into adjusting to divorce rather than into denying it.

To explain how final divorce is, make it clear that you and your ex-spouse will not remarry each other. Also tell your children that divorce is an adult matter like other adult decisions, and that there is nothing that the children can do to change things. You might find it useful to compare your decision to other decisions you have made on behalf of the family.

Here is one example of an explanation that the divorce is final: "Remember when we said good-bye to Aunt Jean? We didn't want her to leave, but it was her decision to move to Denver. That's a grown-up decision.

"Divorce is like that. It's a decision that adults make, and the children can't do anything about it. I know you want us to get back together again, but that's not going to happen.

"There's nothing you can do about it. You might think that if you are really good or really bad, we'll be together again. But you didn't make the decision in the first place, so you can't change it now. We aren't going to change our minds. It's final."

anything else in the world. If all their friends' families are intact, these children feel different, almost as if they belong to another species. They suddenly feel as if they don't belong.

Other children feel embarrassed because they view the failure of the marriage as a reflection on them. They may imagine that everyone else can see what terrible kids they are to make a parent leave them.

Like children in denial, kids who are embarrassed may pretend that the marriage is still intact. They may go to great lengths to avoid letting friends know about the divorce. Eventually, they may withdraw from their friends altogether.

It's not always easy to tell when a child feels embarrassed, so a gentle, direct question is needed. To ease your child's sense of shame, mention your own embarrassment. For instance, you might say, "It was hard for me to tell Grandma that we were getting a divorce. I felt so embarrassed. Do you ever feel that way?"

Another way to help your child cope with embarrassment is to plan social activities with other families of divorce. You might meet other divorced adults at a self-help group. By sharing family activities with them, you can teach your children that they aren't the only ones who come from divorced families. Some schools also offer support groups for children of divorce. These groups meet on a regular basis and help children feel less alone.

## Self-Blame

Another typical reaction children have is to blame themselves for ending the marriage. Feeling guilty may be more comforting to them than feeling helpless. By blaming themselves, children put themselves in positions of power. "If my bad behavior caused the divorce in the first place, then my good behavior can bring my parents back together," they assume.

You may not realize that your child feels responsible unless you ask directly. Many parents report being stunned to discover, years later, that their children felt responsible for the divorce. Some children try to protect their parents by not expressing their feelings, desperately trying not to rock the boat at a difficult point in their parents' lives. Other children don't let anyone know that they blame themselves because they are so ashamed over having done whatever they imagine they did to cause the divorce.

Children need to hear that they are not at fault. This is true even if the couple separated over child-rearing issues. After all, other parents differ over the same issues but do not divorce. Acknowledge that the two of you argued about the children, but that you also quarreled over other issues. Stress that there is nothing the child can do to fix the marriage.

## Grief

When parents separate, children experience a loss, even though the noncustodial parent may still live nearby. They have lost not only their parent's presence, but also a way of life and a sense of togetherness. In many ways, this loss is comparable to a death, and grief is a natural response.

Telling children not to cry or refusing to answer their questions and pushing them to be "grown up" only suppresses grief temporarily. Unresolved grief may emerge as serious problems later.

To work through the grief, children of divorce will exhibit the same behaviors as children mourning a death. They may cry or become preoccupied with the noncustodial parent. That parent's belongings, which once seemed trivial, suddenly become important to the children. Children may wear some article of jewelry or clothing that belonged to an ex-spouse. Others will repeat a favorite phrase of the noncustodial parent to reassure themselves.

Many children act out their loss in play. Some children cast a doll in the role of noncustodial parent, playing house with the

doll over and over again. This type of play actually can be helpful. Each time they play, they find it a little easier to stand the pain of losing a parent.

Children who constantly ask the same questions are filling a similar need. The questions may seem repetitious, but hearing the answers again and again comforts your child, much like a familiar nursery rhyme.

Not all children instinctively know how to comfort themselves in this way. You can help them grieve by occasionally crying in front of them instead of hiding your tears. Hold your children as they cry, and ask questions that let them express grief. For instance, you might ask, "Do you miss Daddy? What do you miss most?"

## Fear of Abandonment

Separation can be frightening for children because they are so dependent on their parents. Young children especially are terrified over separation, because they haven't developed a sense of time yet. Toddlers can't understand waiting until the weekend to see the noncustodial parent who used to be home every day. Children who fly into a rage or have a crying fit each time an adult leaves are saying how afraid they are of being left alone.

If you initiated the divorce because of your ex-spouse's objectionable behavior, your children also may assume that you will abandon them eventually. "If Daddy got rid of Mommy when she was bad, he'll get rid of me, too," they reason. To reassure themselves, they may test the rules the parent has set—constantly—or so it might seem to the custodial parent who now must bear the entire burden of setting limits.

Most children resolve their abandonment fears once life after divorce finds its own rhythm. As children see that Daddy will keep them even if they've been bad, they feel less need to act up. When they realize that Mommy does indeed visit them every weekend and can be called on the phone anytime, they understand that Mommy has not abandoned them.

But children who don't resolve these abandonment fears may have lingering problems in relationships. They may be wary of forming any attachments for fear of being left behind. They may enter into relationships, but test the relationship relentlessly to see if the other person will abandon them. Children who still seem to have abandonment fears long after the divorce may profit from the support of a professional counselor.

## Loyalty Conflicts

Friends of a newly divorced couple often wonder whether their friendship with one person will interfere with their friendship with the other. Children feel much the same conflict: They long to remain loyal to both parents but feel caught between them.

Many children feel that way because each parent gives them the message, "If you love me, you'll take my side." When the children are visiting the noncustodial parent, they feel compelled to paint a grim picture of the custodial parent; when they are back at home with the custodial parent, they pretend that they did not enjoy the visit.

No child can bear that stress for long without developing resentment. You may still feel angry at your ex-spouse or feel that you both are competing for the child's love. You also may feel rejected or abandoned each time your child leaves. It isn't easy to give your child permission to continue loving the other parent, but it can be one of the most supportive moves you can make for your child.

To help children maintain their ties to the other parent, you can:

- support your ex-spouse's decisions;
- encourage your child to keep the visitation schedule;
- avoid making the child a go-between;
- work out problems directly with your ex-spouse, out of the child's earshot.

## Taking Care of Yourself

Many of the problems kids experience mimic their parents' pain. For instance, children of depressed parents are more likely to be depressed. Kids take their cues from what they see; they handle stress the same way their role models do.

But even if your children don't exactly reflect your own problems, you will find the kids easier to handle if you have taken care of your own needs. After divorce, taking care of yourself may seem impossible, but it's imperative.

Your mental health is linked to physical well-being: Getting enough sleep and eating a proper diet are essential. A regular fitness routine can give you more energy, improve your outlook, and be a source of new friends. Join a health club or exercise with friends. Thirty minutes of vigorous exercise three times a week provides cardiovascular fitness and helps you maintain the proper weight. Staying in shape not only gives you energy, but also builds your self-image and thus improves your outlook on life.

Another way to bolster your outlook is to make some uninterrupted time for yourself every day. It can be as simple as a long relaxing bath or a walk in the park at lunch, but that time alone helps you maintain a sense of balance.

Maintaining and renewing your interests can give you a new sense of purpose and energy, too. By starting up a hobby or getting back to an old one, you'll increase your self-esteem. You'll also have more to discuss with your new friends. By taking classes or joining a club in your area, you can meet others who share your interests.

Support systems are essential at this time. Develop and stay in touch with a wide circle of friends and relatives. If you are the custodial parent, you may find that a baby-sitting cooperative is a low-cost way to allow you some time away from the children, safe in the knowledge that the children are in good hands.

Another source of support is a self-help group. Usually such groups are organized by people with similar concerns who meet to discuss common issues and help members feel less alone. Some programs are fairly structured and follow a prescribed series of steps. Others are more flexible about the options you have in rebuilding your life.

Most towns offer single-parent groups or support groups for those who are recently divorced. You might also find companionship in a parenting group or an organization for spouses of substance abusers. Churches, YMCAs, YWCAs, and social welfare agencies can direct you to appropriate groups.

Many people also get a fresh start through therapy. In the months after a divorce, it's comforting to talk with a counselor who knows you well but can maintain enough emotional distance to offer assistance.

To find a therapist who has experience with divorced clients, check in your telephone directory for family therapists, or contact the American Association for Marriage and Family Therapy. Ask friends, physicians, and ministers for recommendations. If finances are a problem, look for a therapist who charges fees according to a sliding scale based on income. Some health insurance plans also cover therapy.

Taking care of yourself physically, intellectually, and emotionally benefits both you and your children. They'll have a parent they can be proud of, and they will trust your advice more if they see that you have your own act together. By making time to take care of yourself, you'll have more to offer them, too.

# DISCIPLINE

There are very few topics that arouse as much concern in parents as discipline. Even intact families find the range of theories on discipline overwhelming. Should you be authoritarian? Permissive? In-between? Should you spank, scold, or ignore? Should you discuss every rule or simply put your foot down?

Unfortunately, such child-rearing issues do not get any easier after a divorce. If anything, discipline becomes even more difficult as children react to the change and each parent has to handle daily situations alone.

Many children are angry at the parent who has moved out, but they direct that anger toward the parent who is still available at home. Children also feel insecure after divorce and test parental authority more than usual to see if the parent is still secure in his or her role as parent. If the parents continue to be gentle but firm with them, gradually kids begin to feel more secure in their new lives.

Children's reactions aren't the only reason that discipline becomes difficult, however. The sheer exhaustion of running a single-parent household can lead parents to give in to children. Some parents also feel overwhelmed at assuming the role of disciplinarian for the first time; others feel the burden of being the only one around to enforce the rules. In addition, parents often feel guilty over the divorce and attempt to make it up to their children by easing up on their controls. Loneliness after divorce also can make parents long for their children's companionship, so some parents go to great lengths to avoid any conflict that might distance their children from them.

All of these reactions are normal, but they can be changed. Researchers have found that the most effective discipline techniques work well for both intact and divorced families. Children seem to respond best to discipline when parents:

- establish clear, enforceable rules;
- explain the reasons for the rules;
- specify the consequences of breaking rules;
- enforce the rules consistently;
- provide liberal amounts of praise and affection.

Implementing these ideas will help your family run more smoothly and will let family members feel more secure.

## Establishing Clear, Enforceable Rules

Many parents have trouble with discipline because they don't adhere to the same set of rules day in and day out. Some of these parents establish too few rules; other parents keep changing the rules; and still others enforce the rules one day, but not the next day. Any of those patterns can be frightening to children.

All children feel more secure when they know what their parents expect of them. By setting clear rules and enforcing them, you let your children know what types of behavior are—or are not—acceptable. Once your children understand these limits, they begin to sense that some things in life are predictable. That doesn't mean that they will obey every rule every time. However, they will feel more comfortable and behave more appropriately because they can rely on you to let them know when they are out of line.

Children also are more likely to behave well if they know the limits ahead of time. If you can anticipate new situations and provide rules before your children encounter new settings, they will have the information they need to behave appropriately.

For instance, imagine that you have read to your son at home, but have never taken him to the library. Before you go to the library together for the first time, you might explain that people will be studying inside. Then you might list three rules: whisper, walk, and turn the book pages without folding or tearing them. By preparing your son, you help him enter the library with confidence. Instead of overreacting to the strange new environment, he knows what to expect.

Teaching kids what you expect is only part of the key to good behavior, though. Equally important is being sure they understand the rules. Although their parents tell them rules, many children feel that life is an endless game in which they must guess at good behavior.

This happens because most parents set rules using broad, vague terms. They say, "Be nice to your brother," or "Act like a gentleman," or "Be neat." Children who honestly think they are following the rules often are surprised to be punished for not measuring up to their parents' unspecified expectations.

A little girl may think she's "being nice" to her brother because she isn't hitting him, only to find that her father expects her to share her toys. A young boy may assume that he's being a gentleman because he is all dressed up, when his mother considers eating with his fork as the standard. An adolescent girl may consider her room perfectly neat because the bed is made, while her father sees only the piles of dirty laundry on the floor.

All these parents could have made the rules clearer and easier to follow by saying what they expect their children to *do*, instead of what they expect them to *be*. You should be able to tell the child what actions you expect to see when the child is obeying the rule. If children know what actions you expect, they will know immediately if they have broken the rule. They may not agree with the rule, but they will know how to keep it.

In each pair of rules below, the first rule is vague and open to interpretation; the second rule clearly states what behavior the parent expects to see.

- "Dress appropriately for the restaurant."
- "Wear a dress shirt and tie. No jeans."

- "Put more effort into your homework."
- "Use an eraser instead of scratching out your mistakes."

- "Be on your best behavior at the theater."
- "Walk in the aisles and don't talk during the play."

- "Get ready for school."
- "Put on your clothes and put your books near the front door."

Another key to good rules is making them enforceable. If a rule is rarely or never enforced, the children begin to lose respect not only for that rule, but also for their parent. When you set a rule, you should anticipate that it will be broken, so it should be a rule you can enforce consistently. The acid test for enforceable rules is: Will you know every time that your child breaks the rule, without depending on other people's testimony? If not, then it's not enforceable.

## Explain the Reasons For the Rules

Children are more likely to follow rules that are reasonable. Arbitrary rules, often set in the heat of the moment, are more apt to be broken. One way to guard against setting arbitrary rules is to make a habit of explaining the reasons for any new rules you set. When you take the time to explain a rule, you can see if it sounds reasonable to you.

Most rules can be explained in terms of their effect on the child or on other people. For instance, you can explain waiting for a green light by saying, "You might get hit by a car if you cross on red." When you assign one child to wash the dishes, you can explain that everyone in the family has some job to perform so that no one has to do everything.

Giving reasons for rules does not mean that you have to defend the rules at length, however. A simple explanation is all that's needed to show that there is some reason behind the rule.

Once you've explained the reason, it's best to refuse to enter into a debate over the rule, because most debates are only power struggles. Most children will argue about some rules in an effort to test your seriousness. By quietly steering away from such arguments, you'll demonstrate more commitment to your position than an argument ever could. In the process, you'll also help your children know that the limits are firm and that you're in control as leader of the house. This will help them feel more secure.

## Specifying the Consequences

Telling children the consequences of breaking the rules is as important as setting them. It lets them know what to expect. Most children have a strong sense of fairness. When you stipulate the consequences as you're establishing the rule—before the child even has a chance to break the rule—you can appeal to your child's sense of fairness if the rule is broken later.

If you have stated the rule and its consequence clearly, children sense that you've given them fair warning. On the other hand, if you give a clear rule but no consequence, the children may be stunned when you apply a consequence they never expected. Providing a consequence ahead of time also prevents you from flying off the handle and applying an arbitrary punishment when you're angry.

Consequences should be just as specific as rules are. Warnings such as "You'll be sorry" are merely threats that tease the child into disobeying you. Warnings such as "If you don't put your bike away, you won't be able to ride it the next time you want to" let the child know exactly what action you will take if the rule is broken.

## Enforcing the Rules Consistently

Any rule you make should be important enough to enforce consistently. By enforcing a rule every time it's broken, you continue to provide your children with a sense that life is predictable and that you can be trusted to do what you say you will. Inconsistency in enforcing rules seems unfair and frightening to children.

Most rules fall into two categories: task rules and social rules. Task rules specify a job or chore to be carried out. To enforce task rules:

- set a time limit;
- supervise or check to see that the task has been completed;
- provide praise, smiles, hugs, or other rewards when the job is done;
- ignore irrelevant behavior such as complaints, grimaces, and tantrums;
- if the job is not done within the time limit, apply the consequence you already established.

Social rules teach consideration for others, such as waiting one's turn to talk or not hitting the baby. To enforce social rules:
- provide praise, smiles, hugs, or other rewards when your child obeys the rule;
- ignore irrelevant behavior such as complaints, grimaces, and tantrums;
- ignore misbehavior unless it is dangerous, other people are responding inappropriately to it, or your child gets pleasure out of it. Apply immediate consequences in one of these situations.

## Offer Liberal Amounts of Praise and Affection

All too often parents forget to use one of the most powerful disciplinary tools at their disposal: their approval. Children crave attention and reassurance, and even the most confident youngsters appreciate hearing that you noticed their good behavior.

In addition to approval, rewards can be extremely helpful. It's not necessary to use rewards for every instance of good behavior, though. Save the rewards to use in special situations—for instance, when a new behavior is very difficult for your child, or when your child is very young.

If you do use a material reward such as a toy, treat, or sticker, be sure to offer your praise before you give the child the prize. By saying "I really appreciate the way you hung up your coat right away" before you give your son a plastic dinosaur, you help him attach importance to your praise. Gradually, as he becomes more consistent in hanging up his coat, he will have less need for dinosaurs and will put the coat away for the simple reward of your praise.

Since children are eager to earn your affection, in most instances they will continue a behavior if you have cheered them on when they first learned the behavior. If you want to teach your daughter to touch her baby brother gently, immediately smile at her and tell her exactly what she did right: "Joey really likes it when you kiss him. I'm proud of you for being so gentle with him." To help her learn this more quickly, praise her every time she is gentle.

The name of the game is "Catch the children being good." The more often you can spot your children behaving appropriately, and immediately praise them for it, the more likely they are to continue behaving well in the future.

"Praise" may seem fairly vague to you, but we all have felt the warmth of someone's approval. Watch your children to see how they react to different kinds of approval. Some children can go for hours on a compliment, while others get a big charge out of shaking your hand. Still others like nothing better than a hug.

## Discipline and Your Ex-Spouse

In an ideal situation, both you and your ex-spouse would agree on rules for the children and would use the same consequences when the children broke the rules. However, it's not essential to agree, although life is much simpler when you do. What's important is to support your ex-spouse's decisions about rules. That means expecting your children to follow the rules in each household and confining any discipline disagreements you and your ex-spouse may have to yourselves.

That doesn't mean that you must enforce rules in the same way as your ex-spouse, although it certainly makes life easier when you can. It does mean that each of you must be consistent in enforcing rules every time the child breaks them, using whatever consequence you've established in your own particular household. Children can understand the concept of different rules and different consequences in two households, much as they understand that different teachers will have different rules and consequences.

For instance, your teenagers may have to come home earlier at night when they visit their father. In addition, he might enforce their curfew by telling them that they must do five minutes of chores for every five minutes they are late. You, on the other hand, might enforce your teenagers' curfews by telling the kids that they must come home early the next night whenever they violate their curfew.

It would be easier if you and your ex-husband could agree on curfew, but that's not the most important thing. It is important that you each support the other's rules and consequences. Although you disagree with your ex-spouse, you'll make things easier on him by simply telling your kids, "When you're at your dad's, you have to follow his rules, and when you're here, you have to follow mine."

## Ways to Praise Your Children

Most adults get bored when they hear the same compliments over and over, and children are no different. If you're looking for new ways to show your approval or give rewards, consider these:

**Nonverbal signs:**
- smiles
- "OK" sign
- hugs
- tickling
- "Gimme five!"
- lifting your child high in the air
- winks
- "thumbs up" sign
- gold stars on a chart
- applause
- stickers
- smiley face stamped on one hand
- dancing with your child

**Verbal:**
- "Thank you."
- "Wow!"
- "I really like it when . . ."
- "A masterpiece!"
- "All by yourself?"
- "Terrific!"
- "You're such a big help."
- "I knew I could count on you."
- "Top-notch!"
- "That was so thoughtful of you."
- "First-rate!"
- "Wonderful!"
- "Fantastic!"
- "You did a super job!"

**Privileges and activities:**
- reading an extra story
- staying up later
- watching a special TV show
- renting a videotape
- going to the park or zoo
- using colored marking pens
- getting an ice-cream cone
- baking together
- listening to a special record
- calling grandparents/friends
- going swimming, skating, sledding
- having a picnic with you
- sleeping in a sleeping bag
- dressing up in your clothes
- playing a game with you
- being excused from a chore
- sleeping later than usual
- using the car
- having a later curfew than usual

# AS YOUR CHILD GROWS

## Your Infant

**Children of different ages tend to have different responses to divorce. In this section, we'll explore some of these responses to help you and your children work through them. We'll also offer suggestions for activities you can share, tips on discipline, and books on divorce for kids.**

Your mental health and adjustment to divorce are the most important influences on an infant. Although babies may not remember a divorce later, they do feel its stress. Prolonged tension during pregnancy can make the baby irritable. If the parent then has to raise the newborn child alone, the stress can seem overwhelming. To counteract the stress, you need to take care of yourself as best you can (see page 15).

The baby's earliest attachments may influence later relationships. You may not have the time or energy to give your infant enough attention. Children who are ignored as babies sometimes go to extremes as adults: They may cut themselves off from others or have an insatiable appetite for attention. If you are concerned that your baby won't get enough attention, ask relatives and friends to play with the baby. Some towns also offer drop-in centers for parents and children. The parents can enjoy the company of other adults while their children participate in play groups and structured activities.

Instead of ignoring the baby, some parents experience the opposite problem. They compensate for the loss of a spouse by focusing all their energies on the baby. As a result, the baby feels no need to develop independence. By parenting too much, these parents deny their children the rest they need and encourage them to be clingy.

If you think that you may be overparenting, schedule activities for yourself. If baby-sitting is a problem, simply schedule some time at home for calling relatives or having friends in for pizza. Distracting yourself with the company of friends is a good antidote to overparenting.

### Activities for The Two of You

Try some of these activities to entertain the baby and help both of you relax.

- Touch the baby in different ways: Stroke the side of the face, play "This-Little-Piggy" with the toes, and blow on the stomach.
- Give the baby something to look at. Make faces or hold the baby before the mirror. Display bright colors.
- Take a walk and point out the sights as if you were a tour guide. Bad weather? Go to the mall.
- Play pulling, pushing, and grasping games with bright toys or shiny spoons. Try squeeze toys, too.
- Let the baby hear different sounds: the hair dryer, vacuum cleaner, and nursery rhymes you recite.

# Your Toddler

Though their parents view toddlers as tiny, vulnerable creatures, children between the ages of 1 and 3 certainly don't see themselves that way. They have become independent with awesome speed, learning to walk, talk, and feed themselves in a few short months. Eager to piece the world together, toddlers notice everything parents do—sometimes to their parents' chagrin.

Therefore, it's a mistake to assume that toddlers can't understand divorce. Unlike younger siblings, toddlers know when someone important to them is gone, and they miss them terribly. True, toddlers may be puzzled over the word "divorce" and may ask questions that mystify their parents, but they do have a basic understanding that one parent no longer lives in the house. It may take every bit of your patience to explain and re-explain the separation, but your toddler deserves to know what's happened.

Still, even the best explanation can't take the pain away. Many toddlers signal their unhappiness with regression, separation anxiety, or increased aggression.

## Regression

Establishing independence is hard work—so hard that all toddlers are tempted to give it up at times. Parents in the happiest of homes notice that the child who relinquished the pacifier one week suddenly screams for it the next. After an illness or other stress, toddlers are even more likely to revert to familiar behavior—after all, it served them just fine for a long time and it feels safe.

Divorce also makes kids regress. By this age, they have learned to trust adults. But divorce gives them the message that adults can't always be trusted. People who cheered the child's every move now seem too distracted to notice. One of the most important people in the toddler's life is no longer around as much. Their established daily routine has been upset by the divorce, and young children cherish their routines.

Angry and frightened, many toddlers search for something to comfort themselves. The return to earlier behaviors seems like an old familiar blanket. Besides, if they go back to being babies, their parents will *have* to come together to take care of them again, these tots reason.

Not all toddlers choose the same way to regress. Some will abandon any semblance of toilet training, others will refuse to feed themselves, and still others demand a return to the bottle they haven't used in months. Parents who patiently accept the setback but gently prod the child back to independence find that the regression is short-lived. In addition, repeated assurances that you still love them and will take care of them help most toddlers realize that independence isn't so scary.

Another way to help re-establish your toddler's trust is to make only those promises you know you can keep. When toddlers see that they can count on you to keep your word, they begin to feel comfortable again.

It's also important to be consistent with discipline. Toddlers need to feel that you won't fall apart when they disobey. They need to know that you are still the same firm parent you've always been.

## Separation Anxiety

Any parent who has left a screaming child with a sitter knows the terror of separation anxiety all too well. Toddlers may demand their independence, but deep down, they're scared to death of being left alone. With no sense of time, toddlers can't imagine when or even if parents will ever return from a night at the movies or a day at work.

Toddlers in the midst of a divorce feel that their worst nightmare has come true. One parent really has left the house; what's to prevent that other parent from leaving them to fend for themselves?

## Activities for the Two of You

Toddlers are wonderful little people who give adults license to be kids again. Take advantage of that fact and enjoy your 1- to 3-year-old. Try some of these simple pastimes.

- Go to the park. Toddlers can spend endless amounts of time swinging, climbing, and running. Bring a large ball along for even more fun. You'll be exhausted long before they will, but you'll both sleep well that night.
- Read. Children of this age love to cuddle up in your lap for a story, and they're easily pleased. They want to hear the same story over and over again. Try using different voices for the characters, and ask your child to tell you about the pictures.
- Play with water or sand. Let your child stand on a stool at the kitchen or bathroom sink and splash away. Pouring water into and out of plastic cups, bowls, and strainers is another favorite game. In warmer weather, use the same supplies in the sand.
- Build. Younger children are happy making towers of plastic storage containers or stacking blocks and knocking them down again. Older tots can enjoy building with large interlocking plastic blocks.
- Play children's music. Cassettes of children's songs and nursery rhymes can provide hours of fun. Most children will dance at the drop of a hat, and they don't care if you have two left feet. Try such favorites as "The Hokey Pokey"; or have a parade, marching in time to the music.

Faced with that thought, it's no wonder that some toddlers react to divorce with such fear. You may find that your child refuses to go to bed, and then once in bed, screams and cries to the point of exhaustion. Bedtime seems dangerous to them: They worry that you may sneak off and leave the minute they close their eyes. Nightmares, typical to children of this age, may intensify, reflecting the loss of control the toddler feels.

Other separations may also become scary. Children who have been attending a day-care center happily for months may put up a fight each morning as you leave them. Baby-sitters are equally frightening.

But you can hardly lock yourself in the house just to help your children. You can comfort them best by establishing predictable comings and goings that the child can depend on. Regular meals together and traditional bedtime rituals help toddlers understand that they can count on your presence during certain routines. Don't scold them for their feelings, but patiently reassure them you will return, without giving in to their misbehavior.

## Aggression

Toddlers can be lots of fun. They also can be fiercely independent. Parents dread the notorious "terrible twos"—the screaming tantrums, the foot-stomping, the piercing cry of "It's mine!" Isn't there a more pleasant way to reach the age of 3?

Not for most healthy toddlers. Few children reach independence without trying to put their parents in their place. And children of divorce are no different, though they may prolong this stage beyond anyone's patience.

Most toddlers aren't sophisticated enough to explain their feelings beyond the tantrum of the minute. It's not easy to watch, but

# Your Toddler

## Discipline Tip: Time-Out

When your toddler misbehaves to the extent that discipline is needed, try using "time-out." By isolating the child with no toys nearby, both you and your toddler get a chance to regroup. During this break, most children can think of something else to do once the "time-out" is over.

When you call a time-out, firmly say to your child, "You hit Dan. Time-out." Then send or take the child to a spot away from other people or sources of amusement. You might use an entryway, a special chair, or a corner of the room. For the next few minutes, everyone is to ignore the child, no matter how loud the protests. Don't respond to your child in any way, and don't look in that direction. If you are busy with your own activities, your child will get interested enough to calm down and will want to join you when time-out is over.

Begin timing only after your child is quiet. When your child has been quiet for several minutes (about one minute for each year of your child's age), say, "OK, time-out is over." Then return to your normal routine without scolding the child.

The first few times you use time-out, explain, "Time-out means I am not going to talk to you and you cannot talk to me. When you have calmed down, we can start over. You have to be quiet for a few minutes before you can come out of time-out." Children who won't go to time-out or who get up before time-out is over should be restrained. Usually, a gentle but firm hand on the shoulder is all that's needed. Gradually, your child will show an understanding of time-out by going right to the time-out area and sitting down without these directions.

increased aggression at this age may simply be your child's way of saying, "I'm angry. How could you do this to me?"

Aggression couldn't come at a worse time for the guilt-ridden parents who've been torturing themselves, wondering how they could do what they are doing to their child. Yet the anger deserves to be heard; it's perfectly natural for a child to be furious when parents separate, and anger may continue for several months until the child is again secure with you and your ex-spouse. Telling children, "Stop crying," or "Don't get mad," only cuts off the anger exactly when children should express it. In fact, children who act out their anger as toddlers often have the best adjustment to divorce in the long run.

But accepting the child's anger doesn't mean that you have to tolerate kicking, hitting, and biting. You can acknowledge your child's anger with responsive listening, but apply the same consequences you have always used for misbehavior.

Actually, your toddler is looking for exactly that consistency and strength in you. Children who see that you are still in charge and that there are still limits to their behavior will be less frightened when their anger gets out of their control. When they know that they can expect the same consequences for slapping that they got before the divorce, they begin to feel that life might return to normal.

## Books for Your Toddler

*Mom and Dad Don't Live Together Any More.* Stinson, Kathy. Willowdale, Ontario: Annick Press, 1984.

*Please Come Home.* Sanford, Doris. Portland, Ore.: Multnomah Press, 1985.

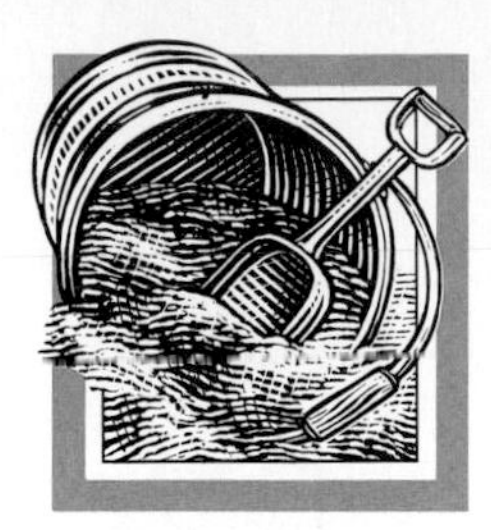

AS YOUR CHILD GROWS

# Your Preschooler

By the age of 3, children have a lot to be proud of, and they don't hesitate to tell you that. Most kids consider themselves the center of the universe and are puzzled when others don't share that opinion.

Children at this age are quite imaginative and act out their fears and hopes in dramatic play. By observing their play, you may learn what's troubling a child who finds feelings hard to express. Typically, preschoolers react with sadness, anger, excessive responsibility, or self-blame.

## Sadness

Preschoolers already have formed strong attachments to their parents and certainly know when the family has changed. Because they haven't developed a strong sense of time yet, they are less likely to understand how permanent divorce is, but it makes them very sad, nonetheless. Young children may feel rejected by the non-custodial parent, especially if the divorce hasn't been explained as a decision between two adults.

Some preschoolers express their sorrow by withdrawing or becoming listless. They may sit on the sidelines during group activities at preschool or mope around the house, showing no interest in friends and siblings. Others express sadness through their art or through play.

However, most preschoolers cry long and often. They cry because they miss the noncustodial parent. They also cry because they miss the amount of time and attention the custodial parent used to provide.

Children also mourn the loss of other attachments. Some children find that divorce suddenly deprives them of cherished grandparents. Others see their siblings becoming more distant—either because the other children are sorting out their own feelings, or because the other ones have taken sides in the divorce, perhaps supporting the noncustodial parent.

Although you may regret the pain the divorce has caused them, you can best help your children by minimizing your guilt and allowing them to be sad. At this age, children don't have the words to express why they are sad, so tears are their only outlet. Telling a preschooler not to cry merely confuses the child, who wonders why tears seem to well up even though crying is a no-no. Try to just listen to the feelings without defending the divorce. Give your child some time to cry in your arms or with a favorite stuffed animal.

You also can minimize some sadness if you explain and re-explain the divorce without giving any indication that one parent is rejecting the child. Saying "We will always love you" can help children understand that parents are rejecting one another, not them.

Sadness should be considered normal and healthy unless it persists for months. In that case, get professional help.

## Anger

Along with sorrow may come anger. Most children will be furious with one or both parents for breaking up the family unit. Often children are especially angry with the parent who moves out of the house. However, because they are with the custodial parent most of the time, they direct most of their anger toward that parent.

Preschoolers are especially likely to act out their anger because they know no other way to express it. They may act out anger by becoming the neighborhood bully. They throw food at friends, topple a classmate's stack of blocks, or clobber an innocent bystander. They also may return to the "terrible twos," although they are well past that age.

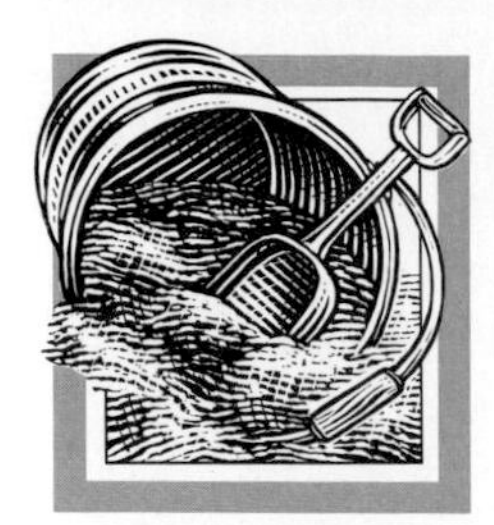



# Your Preschooler

Some children turn their anger inward. Afraid to be angry openly, they may hurt themselves. Some children become depressed and express a low opinion of themselves.

At this age, kids have vivid imaginations, and they may alarm their parents with their violent play. But games of slaying dragons, shooting rustlers, or stabbing burglars are their way of expressing and conquering fear.

You can help your youngster through this difficult period by allowing some normal, healthy outlets for aggression. Resist your own impulses to be overprotective. Instead, cheer your daughter on as she climbs to the top of the jungle gym. Urge your son to jump into the pool. Let them try riding two-wheelers as soon as they show interest. Allow them plenty of time to be active.

Even though anger is healthy and aggression is normal, you shouldn't ignore inappropriate behavior. Kids learn good behavior only when they have limits, so maintain the consequences you normally use for misbehavior. If you've always sent your son to time-out for kicking, continue to do so. You can explain, "It's OK to be angry, but it's not OK to kick. Kicking hurts."

## Excessive Responsibility

After a divorce, some children suddenly become docile and cooperative. They take on chores willingly and with a minimum of direction when asked to do so. In fact, some children stun their parents by offering to help before they are even asked. For a newly single parent who feels overwhelmed by the demands of life after divorce, this behavior comes as a relief.

Children who become "little adults" after divorce may seem to be coping rather well. But most of them are miserable. Some may be trying to become invisible so that no one can find them and hurt them again. They also may be taking over for the noncustodial parent. In fact, many of them have been told, "You're the man (or woman) of the house now."

"Little adults" may be helpful to their parents, but their sense of responsibility can be overdone. Children need to learn to play; if they assume adult roles too early, they'll be deprived of the creative and social skills they should be developing at this time. Those who miss out on childhood may become resentful, immature adults.

If your child seems to be taking on too much responsibility, you can help. Redirect your child's energies by suggesting other things to do. If your child seems reluctant to play alone or with friends, you can encourage play by joining in the fun yourself. Your local recreation department also may offer activities or supervised playgrounds that will interest your child.

It's easy to express too much enthusiasm for "little adults," but it's important to tone down your appreciation for hard work. Try to praise your "little adults" for playing together, for being creative in their play, and for entertaining themselves.

## Self-Blame

Some children's extremely good behavior isn't a way to become invisible or take over the noncustodial parent's role. Instead, it reflects a sense of guilt. Most kids develop a conscience at this age, but some kids take it to extremes. Since they think everything revolves around them, they hold themselves responsible for everything that happens, even if it had little to do with them. This makes them feel powerful in a world that usually makes them feel powerless.

Preschoolers are beginning to develop the notion of cause and effect, though they don't always connect the right cause and effect. If your daughter notices the sun move, she may conclude that the sun is following her. If you feel your son's feverish forehead, when he gets better, he may reason that you took the fever away.

## Discipline Tip: Ignoring

Your attention is one of the most powerful rewards a preschooler can imagine, so young children will make strenuous efforts to catch your eye. When you pay attention, you reinforce their behavior, which makes them more likely to try it again. Unfortunately, you can reinforce bad as well as good behavior with your attention.

That's why ignoring works so well in eliminating misbehavior. When you ignore misbehavior, preschoolers will seek another way to get attention. If you notice them again as soon as they behave well, they see that misbehaving won't pay off but behaving well will.

Of course, you can't ignore dangerous behavior. Neither can you ignore behavior that is rewarding in itself. Each time your daughter steals a toy, she rewards herself with the toy. She doesn't care whether you notice, so ignoring won't stop that behavior. You must apply some other consequence. (See page 39 for an explanation of logical consequences.)

On the other hand, if your daughter tries out some swear words on you, and you react in any way, she'll try them again and again. The words themselves aren't rewarding, but your attention is. If you ignore her when she swears, you'll eliminate the swearing. You must be consistent, though. If you ignore her at some times and not at others, she will keep swearing.

Ignoring misbehavior takes patience because your child's misbehavior may increase initially. She's thinking, "I guess Daddy didn't hear me; I'll try again." However, if you keep ignoring her, you'll see a long-lasting improvement.

Some parents think they're ignoring children when they say, "I'm going to ignore your behavior," but that sentence alone is enough attention to satisfy most children. Instead, try these steps:

- don't answer your child;
- don't look at your child;
- talk to someone else.

Ignoring misbehavior works more quickly if you couple it with praise as soon as your child behaves well. It also works better if you ask other people to ignore the misbehavior.

That's why it's not surprising when preschoolers assume that they caused your divorce. Most children won't tell you that directly unless you ask, because they are too ashamed of the horrible things they imagine they have done to cause the divorce. If you ask, they may explain that you divorced because they spilled their milk, wet the bed, or broke the tape recorder.

But many preschoolers will conclude, "If I made Daddy leave by being bad, I can make him come back by being good." They make strenuous efforts to be helpful, to be quiet, to make up for past mistakes. They make presents in the hopes that their parents will forgive them and love them again.

You can prevent some of this in your initial explanation. You also can prevent some self-blame if you make every effort to tell your children that their other parent still loves them, or if you urge your ex-spouse to tell them that directly. Still, your kids need to hear that your divorce was an adult decision that they couldn't control.

# Your Preschooler

## Activities for the Two of You

Preschool children have boundless energy and are eager to use it. But they also are capable of and need an occasional quiet sit-down game that offers respite to the weary parent.

Most preschoolers have had enough experience to really play with you, not just next to you. So live it up and join right in the fun.

- Fantasy games. Make believe and your child will join right in. Pretend to be lions, tigers, or bears. For a special treat, visit a theatrical supply shop and invest in a few inexpensive costume hats. In an instant, the two of you can become pirates, cowhands, or witches.
- Table games. Kids of this age are ready for simple board games. Lotto, Candyland, and Chutes and Ladders are old favorites. Dominoes come in several varieties—some with dots, others with cartoon characters.
- Drawing and painting. Your child's new ability to sit still opens the door to a wealth of art activities. When crayons have lost their appeal, try washable markers. Most drugstores sell inexpensive starter kits of watercolors. You'll win extra points if you can tolerate the lovely squishy mess of finger paints, which are also available at most drugstores.
- The zoo. It's no secret that preschoolers love animals. If there's no zoo in your area, try a pet store, or feed the birds at your local park.
- Cooking. All that pouring sand in the toddler stage pays off now in the kitchen. Preschoolers can add the cup of sugar, stir the batter, and, of course, sample the results.
- Movies. By this time, kids can sit through the more engrossing movies. Enjoy the classics at your local theater or video store. Share a batch of popcorn for a special treat.

Many children need to hear this again and again until they feel certain that they can't do anything to reunite the two of you.

One way to broach the subject is to tell your kids how common self-blame is. For example, you could say, "Some kids think that they did something wrong that made their parents get a divorce. Do you ever worry about that?" Then you could say, "Divorce is an adult decision. You might think that you did something terrible to make us divorce, but we decided to divorce because we can't live together. You didn't cause the divorce, and you can't change it, either."

## Books for Your Preschooler

*Dinosaurs Divorce: A Guide for Changing Families.* Brown, Laurene Krasny, and Brown, Marc. Boston: Little, Brown, and Co., 1986.

*Sometimes a Family Has to Split Up.* Watson, Jane Werner; Switzer, Robert E.; and Hirshberg, J. Cotter. New York: Crown Publishers, Inc., 1988.

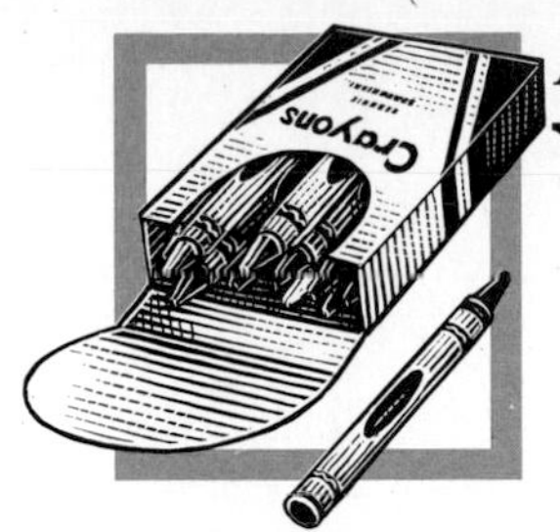


AS YOUR CHILD GROWS

# Your 5- to 8-Year-Old

Between the ages of 5 and 8, children strive to become more independent. Eager to catch up with "the big kids," they focus their energy on learning everything from reading to riding a two-wheeler. They also are starting to reason and can understand the logic behind some rules.

School can enhance the child's feelings of independence and may be a source of solace for a child whose parents are divorcing. On a practical level, school gives children something to focus on besides their family. Most children find the routine of the school day comforting because it offers them something predictable during what may be a time of upheaval at home. The skills children learn in school also make them feel capable and unique. Children of this age still idolize their parents, but they are learning that parents and children can have different talents—and they treasure their own gifts.

Besides teaching children new skills, school offers kids a place to widen their circle of friends, who become more important during these years. Many kids find it reassuring to be able to talk with friends and teachers in addition to parents, who may not always be available, or may be too wrapped up in their own concerns to listen carefully.

Although these children crave independence, they also need role models. At this age, children view adults as superior beings. Youngsters go to great pains to imitate everything adults do; they cannot imagine a parent or teacher failing at anything.

As a result of this mind-set, divorce comes as a great shock to children. Suddenly they must face the fact that their parents aren't always perfect and can make mistakes. They are apt to feel that the rug has been pulled out from under them, and they feel tremendously anxious. They might express their feelings in the form of phobias, fear of the future, or depression.

## Anxiety and Phobias

Although your children are becoming more independent, they know they are still dependent on you. Despite their occasional fantasies of running away, kids don't really believe that they could make it on their own. How would they find a place to live? Where would they get food, and how would they cook it? And how would they even get to school on time without your help?

They may pretend to be bold, but children in the early elementary grades are just as frightened by your separation as their younger siblings are. They may become clingy, refusing to leave your side. They might think, "If I keep my eye on Mommy, she won't leave me like Daddy did."

Some children want to guard you so closely that they refuse to go to school. They may simply say no, or they may develop a variety of illnesses in order to stay home. Either way, the result is the same: If they can manage to stay home, they can keep an eye on you.

You may think that something is desperately wrong at school to make your child want to avoid it so. Although educators call this behavior "school phobia," children who act this way aren't really afraid of school itself. They are scared to death that you will abandon them while they are at school, so they want to stay home to make sure that you don't sneak off. If you are at work, they can't keep an eye on you, so they are relieved if they can make you stay home to take care of them.

Other children keep going to school, but develop physical symptoms that show their anxiety. They may sweat, tremble, develop tics, or have trouble falling asleep. Many children who were doing fine in school begin to slip as their fears interfere with their ability to concentrate.

Adults who have no intention of abandoning their children are genuinely

# Your 5- to 8-Year-Old

## Discipline Tip: Shaping

When you are trying to improve your child's behavior, try a step-by-step approach. Reinforcing a child for each step taken that comes closer to the final goal is called shaping. Because 5- to 8-year-olds crave praise, shaping works very well with them.

You used shaping without even thinking about it when your children were infants. You cheered when they crawled, then when they stood up, and finally when they walked. But many parents forget about shaping when their children are older.

To use shaping, break the desired behavior into tiny steps. The first time the kids do one step completely, praise them. Praise them for every step they add to the first, and continue until they behave as well as you expect or until they perform an entire job.

Try shaping when you assign a new chore. If you want your son to set the table, praise him when he gets forks at each place. When he does that for a few days, praise him for also setting a napkin at each place. When he does that consistently, praise him for putting out the plates, too. Continue until he sets the entire table.

Shaping also works when your child can't take one giant step from misbehavior to improved behavior. If your daughter never cleans her room, she won't suddenly keep it spotless. Use shaping by praising her when she makes the bed; then makes it and hangs up her clothes; then makes it, hangs up her clothes, and picks up her toys. Continue until she routinely keeps the room neat.

Keep forward motion by remembering your goal. Increase your praise each time your child improves. Shaping may be a slow process, but it's more effective and more pleasant than punishing children for misbehavior.

puzzled over these anxieties. But you may understand your children better if you think of your own reaction to your recent loss or separation. You probably experienced some panic, too, wondering "What will I ever do without her?" Imagine how much more frightening that must be for a child, who can't even take care of basic needs without adult assistance.

If your child tries to stay home from school often, discuss it with the teacher. Most schools have had experience with school phobia and have effective techniques for treating it. You may be asked to bring your child to school for just a half-hour at first, gradually lengthening the time until your child can attend for the full day. Or your child may stay at school all day, but be eased into the classroom gradually, spending the rest of the time in the office.

You and the teacher may also find a reward system helpful; for instance, your child might try to earn stickers for getting to school on time, staying in class for an hour, or staying for an entire morning. Whatever approach you try, it will be most effective if you and the teacher work out a program together.

You also can help anxious children by reassuring them, again and again, that you will always be there for them. Be reliable: Try to be on time whenever you pick the kids up from school or a visitation. Consistency is also important in home routines. Even if you and your ex-spouse have different routines in your separate homes, your children will find it comforting if they know what to expect from each home every time they stay there.

## Telling the Teacher

You might be wondering whether you should tell your children's teachers of your divorce. You may be embarrassed, or you may worry that the teachers' reactions will harm your child. What if the teachers expect the worst? If they expect the worst from your child, won't they get it?

Teachers' expectations can be powerful, but their reactions also can be comforting. If they're forewarned, teachers can be more compassionate when a child's behavior changes. And in most cases, there will be some change; very few children have no reaction to the breakup of a family.

In fact, teachers should worry if they see no change in your child, or if the child immediately improves. Children who suddenly become model students usually are in great pain, trying to cover it up by staying out of trouble. Teachers who know of the divorce rightly view such behavior as a cry for help and can refer your child for supportive services.

Because teachers have worked with other children in pain, they may be quite knowledgeable about services for your child. Take advantage of their experience. If you keep teachers updated on your concerns, they can watch for announcements of support groups, recreational activities, and counseling services for your family.

But teachers are more than referral sources. Because teachers see your child six hours a day, five days a week, they become important figures in your child's life. As your child feels the loss of the traditional family unit, teachers can be supportive. They may use books or filmstrips to discuss divorce and give children a chance to vent their feelings. They also can get children involved in activities that will help them have fun.

## Fear of the Future

Anxiety also can surface for some children whenever they think about the future. These children reason that life has already handed them one big unwanted surprise, so what's to prevent life from dealing them another?

Children may exhibit this fear of the future in a variety of ways. They may have unending questions about appointments and transportation arrangements. They may wander around looking for the noncustodial parent, even though they have been told repeatedly where that parent will be living. They may ask, "What are we going to do?" or "How are we going to live?" time and time again. Nightmares are typical for children who can't face their fears during the day.

Using the increased imagination typical at this age, children experiencing divorce see danger lurking around every corner. They might think of being hurt, imagine you dying, or picture the house catching on fire. Any change can give rise to frightening fantasies, so children may react with terror to the slightest variation in routine.

This fear may center on the noncustodial parent. When children can't see a parent on a daily basis, they worry. Some kids wonder whether the noncustodial parent will get enough to eat. Their imaginations even prompt these youngsters to wonder if the noncustodial parent will die without them.

Other children are less worried about their parents and more worried about their own futures. These youngsters may try to assume the role of the noncustodial parent. A little girl might scold the other children for coming home late; a young boy may try

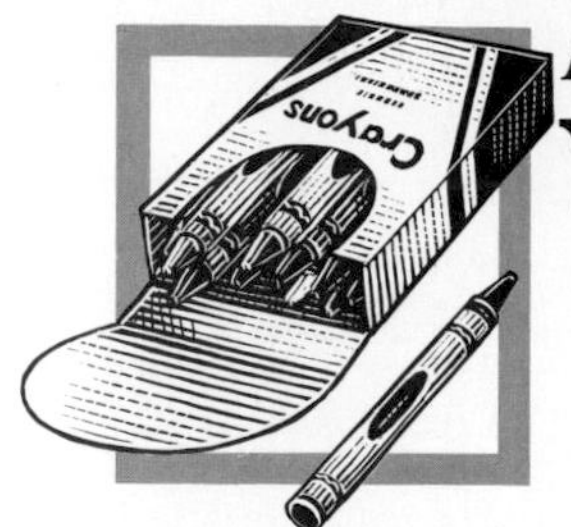




# Your 5- to 8-Year-Old

to protect his mom from burglars. By taking on the parent's role, these children reduce their own anxieties about surviving without the noncustodial parent.

Still other children express their fear directly. They worry aloud that there will be no Christmas gifts. They wonder if there will be enough to eat at home. Some resort to compulsive eating, testing to see just when you will run out of food. By gorging, they are reassuring themselves that there will always be enough food for them. They also eat to fill up the void they feel over losing one parent's presence.

Behind all these worries lurks the children's fear that they will be left alone. One way to cope is to explain child care and visitation arrangements in detail. For instance, you might say, "Mommy is going back to work, and you will be in school during the day. After school, you will stay with Mrs. Boyer until I come home from work. You will see Daddy every weekend, and you can call him on the phone."

If you are the noncustodial parent, you can head off fears by calling the kids frequently. No matter how trivial the calls seem to you, they convince the children you are still alive. It's also reassuring for children to see your new house as soon as possible.

In addition, reassure the children that they will always be taken care of. Most children have wondered what would become of them if they lost one or both parents; if they ask, now is the time to tell them. "If anything ever happened to me, you would move in with Daddy. If anything happened to Daddy, you would move in with Aunt Rita and Uncle Brad." You may worry that the explanation will put ideas in your children's heads, but actually, most children have often considered the possibility of losing both parents. Discussing plans can help them be less afraid of the future.

## Activities for the Two of You

Children between the ages of 5 and 8 love learning something new. They long to imitate adults and will try anything as long as they see you doing it, too. Enjoy that while you can with a few of these activities:

- Visit a museum. Kids really enjoy museums that say, "Please touch." They love to pet animals, push buttons, or sit in the driver's seat of a tractor. Keep your visit short, viewing just two or three rooms. If your child enjoys it, you can return again to see the other rooms.
- Take a nature hike. Bring a jar for catching bugs. Collect leaves or stones and label them later with the help of a book. Look for tracks and guess what animal made them. For a closeup view, bring along a magnifying glass.
- Have a picnic. By this age, your child is old enough to help pack the lunch, and certainly wants a say in the menu. Make the lunch together and tuck in a treat. For a new twist on an old favorite, pack a picnic breakfast and experience the outdoors before the park or beach gets crowded. Too cold or rainy? Hold your picnic indoors. Spread a blanket on the floor in front of the fireplace for a bug-free outing.
- Go swimming. If you don't belong to a health club, check out the free or low-cost public swimming in outdoor pools, neighborhood schools, and university health centers. Most children of this age have conquered any earlier fear of the water and may swim quite well. But even non-swimmers will enjoy splashing, blowing bubbles, or playing water ball.

## Depression

Although preschool children certainly struggle with sadness, older children may feel acutely depressed, like children who have experienced a death in the family. Their grief is deeper because they have a longer history with the noncustodial parent. For five, six, or seven years, they have enjoyed not only a relationship with that parent, but also a fantasy life about that parent. When the noncustodial parent moves out, the children may feel they have to give up dreams of "Dad and me flying airplanes" or "Mom and me appearing in a movie."

Children of this age also are likely to feel that the noncustodial parent has rejected them. They reason, "If Mom moved out, she doesn't love me," and "If my own mother doesn't love me, I must not be lovable."

Some children who become depressed are really quite angry about the divorce. They may have learned to bury their anger or may be afraid to express it for fear of losing the one parent left at home. As a result, they direct the anger at themselves. They criticize themselves harshly, saying, "I'm no good" or "I'm horrible," and they find fault with everything they do. These negative messages further lower their self-esteem.

Children express depression in many ways. They may seem apathetic. Some lose their appetite; others eat incessantly. They may not enjoy school or play and often complain of being bored. Some find it hard to concentrate and feel helpless or hopeless much of the time. They cry readily and are easily frustrated. Mild depression is fairly typical and usually resolved within a few months. You can help mildly depressed children by encouraging them to express their anger or grief and by letting them know you are really there.

If your children were extra dependent on the noncustodial parent before divorce, helplessness may overwhelm them now. Resist the impulse to overprotect them, because that may simply make them dependent on you. These children need the message that they can indeed survive without the other parent. Encourage them when they do something by themselves, and urge them to learn new skills. Enrolling them in a recreation program or letting them take music lessons will give them a renewed sense of competence.

Serious depression also can result in anorexia, drug abuse, or even suicide. Extremely depressed children may imagine suicide as a way of getting back at their parents, not realizing how permanent suicide is. If your child seems very depressed or if the depression lasts for a long time, consult a therapist. You and your child need the support of a trained professional.

### Books for Your 5- to 8-Year-Old

*All Kinds of Families*. Simon, Norma. Niles, Ill.: Whitman, 1976.

*Break-Up*. Padoan, Gianni. Milan, Italy: Child's Play, 1987.

*Dinosaurs Divorce: A Guide for Changing Families*. Brown, Laurene Krasny, and Brown, Marc. Boston: Little, Brown, and Co., 1986.

*Divorce Can Happen to the Nicest People*. Mayle, Peter. New York: Macmillan, 1979.

*I Have Two Families*. Helmering, Doris. Nashville, Tenn.: Abingdon, 1981.

*I Wish I Had My Father*. Simon, Norma. Niles, Ill.: Whitman, 1983.

*Mom Is Dating Weird Wayne*. Auch, Mary Jane. New York: Holiday House, 1988.

*Two Homes to Live In: A Child's-Eye View of Divorce*. Hazen, Barbara Shook. New York: Human Sciences Press, Inc., 1983.

AS YOUR CHILD GROWS

# Your 8- to 12-Year-Old

By the time children reach the preteen years, they have really grown up. Eager to assume responsibility, they may even have paper routes or baby-sitting jobs. They have grown physically and are agile enough to enjoy sports. They thrive on the camaraderie of sports teams and scouting troops.

At the same time, these children long for independence. They have learned the basics of the three R's and are learning to apply those skills. These emotional, physical, and academic capabilities all add up to improved self-esteem. And that, in turn, helps children cope with the turmoil that divorce creates in younger children.

The same kids who enjoy teamwork and scouting are very loyal to their parents. They also are passionate on the subject of fairness and rail against anyone who seems the least bit unfair. And by this time, all their schoolwork is paying off in improved reasoning. This combination of loyalty, a strong sense of fairness, and increased verbal skills can spark many arguments or debates between parent and child.

## Anger

Preteens are apt to be angry about divorce. For years they have idolized their parents; then suddenly they find out that parents can be weak, mean, or vulnerable. Many children feel betrayed. These children often express their disillusionment in anger.

You may be appalled at your children's anger. After all, you never told them you were perfect; in fact, you might remember such phrases as, "Nobody's perfect" or "We all make mistakes." It does no good to protest that, however; whether you told them to or not, your children wanted to believe you were perfect. And they did. Now they feel deceived.

They also feel angry because kids this age see things in black and white. If you told them that marriage is forever, they will be furious when you break your marriage vows. If you taught them not to lie, they will be outraged to find that you had an affair. If you promised to go skiing with them at Christmas, they'll be fuming when you say you won't even be together this Christmas.

Many children have tremendous courage and express their anger in no uncertain terms. Showing kids that you love them despite their anger is one of the best ways to cement family relationships.

This doesn't mean that you should abandon discipline and look the other way when they express anger physically. Children expect consequences for misbehavior; when you give up the consequences you used to administer, they feel uncertain. To help children express anger appropriately, use responsive listening. Show that you understand the feelings, but tell your child, "I know you're angry, but I can't allow you to hit me."

Some children are very angry, but they don't tell their parents. Instead, they direct their anger at others, becoming the neighborhood bully, stealing from friends, or ruining their siblings' possessions. They may try to get back at their parents by playing one against the other or by sabotaging the parents' new relationships.

You may long to put a lid on your kids' anger and deny them any outlet for stormy feelings, but in fact, angry children need to express their anger. However, they need to learn to express anger to the right person at the right time in the right way—a tall order for children who feel out of control. Teach your child to use "I messages" to explain feelings (see page 47). It may take the support of a therapist to help your child feel safe in expressing anger appropriately.

## Loyalty Conflicts

Although conflicting loyalties arise for all children whenever one parent moves out, the pull between two parents is especially painful during the preteen years. Children of this age have learned the value of teamwork. They have had enough experience with friendship to know the pain of betrayal. And preteens have an idealistic

## Adult Role Models

All kids benefit from adults besides their parents who serve as models and confidants. But role models are even more important after a divorce and can be a real comfort to preteens.

Some children hesitate to discuss the divorce at home, fearful that they will hurt or anger their parents. If your children need to express their feelings but can't, another adult can gently ease them into a conversation.

Other adults also can help kids view themselves in a positive light. When you're tired of your kids' arguments, another adult can bring out their sweet side. Role models also can teach your children new skills and hobbies—both of which boost self-esteem.

Many children seek a model to replace the noncustodial parent, especially if the noncustodial parent is the same sex as they are. Boys who live with their mothers and girls who live with their fathers benefit from models they can identify with.

But how do you find a role model? Often kids find their own, "adopting" a friend's parent, talking with a teacher, or visiting a favorite aunt. Grandparents also can be fine models. However, your child may need help to find a good model. The Big Brother and Big Sister organizations provide screened, trained models for children. Other natural models include coaches, ministers, and group leaders.

Be resourceful. You might find a male friend to play with your boys every Sunday. Or you can offer a student dinner in exchange for spending time with your girls. Or you might get your child a volunteer job working under a supervisor who can be a role model.

concept of family loyalty. They stand up for their siblings and parents whenever they feel that the family name is threatened.

When one parent leaves, preteens often feel compelled to take sides. With their black-and-white sense of morality, they assume that one parent is totally guilty, while the other is completely innocent. Parents can make these conflicts even worse. Because preteens can communicate well, parents are tempted to use them as go-betweens. They may ask the child to deliver a message to the ex-spouse. The ex-spouse responds through the child, who is caught in a war of words.

When one parent is angry about the divorce and wants revenge, the child also may be caught in the middle. If the noncustodial parent refuses to pay child support, the custodial parent may refuse to allow the noncustodial parent visitation. Sometimes a parent actively enlists a child's help in getting revenge against the ex-spouse. Parents have even asked their child to spy on the ex-spouse's activities.

Avoid using your child as a go-between. Contact your spouse directly instead. If face-to-face contact is too painful, use the phone or a letter, but *don't* use your children.

Even well-meaning parents test the child's sense of loyalty when they paint their ex-spouse in a bad light. If you divorced your spouse over objectionable behavior, you may worry that your child will wind up acting like the ex-spouse. For instance, if your ex-wife was an alcoholic, you may be tempted to talk about how awful she was, so that your children won't imitate her.

In the end, that strategy backfires. Preteens are apt to side with you because they long for your approval. However, when they reach adolescence and give up the black-and-white, judgmental approach, they may rebel. They may decide that their other parent did have a few good points and that you must have been lying when you portrayed only the bad side. Their trust in you will be destroyed.

To cope with loyalty conflicts, take the middle ground. Preteens are capable of

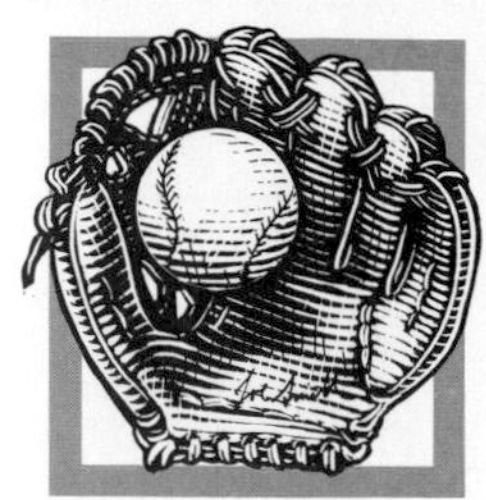



# Your 8- to 12-Year-Old

understanding the reasons for a divorce. With a general account of your reasons, they will be able to understand that you didn't divorce on a whim. Give them some detail in limited quantities. For instance, you might say, "I used to love your mother, but she drinks too much and we can't live together," or "I thought your father was great, but then he fell in love with another woman."

Stop with a limited discussion or you will only make your child bitter. If you feel the need to vent your anger, do it with a friend, not with your child. Therapists also can be useful when you need to vent frustrations and feelings but can't do so in front of the children.

## Loneliness

Many preteens rebel at the idea of having a baby-sitter. "I'm old enough to take care of myself!" they shout. They may be right—many kids of this age can stay alone for part of the day. However, many preteens don't enjoy the experience. Although older teens crave time alone, preteens are more likely to crave company. After a divorce, preteens don't revel in the silence of the house; instead, they miss their parents' company.

Not yet at the rebellious stage, preteens don't consider parents obstacles. The 10-year-old girl who lets herself into an empty house after school may feel that she has lost two good friends: Her exhausted custodial parent has no time for her, and her other parent isn't around much.

She also feels as if she's been pushed too far too soon. While her friends play after school, she has to get dinner ready and set the table. She may have to take care of her little brother, but she feels powerless because he won't listen to her and she can't discipline him. Meanwhile, her mother may have a whole new life, dating and making new friends. Mom's feeling of freedom starkly contrasts with her daughter's feeling of being chained to the house.

Preteens caught in that bind soon begin to resent their custodial parent. They also imagine that life would be much better if only they lived with the other parent. Of course that parent would always be there for them, these preteens fantasize. But preteens who do move to the noncustodial parent's home often find that the loneliness persists. Although changing homes gives them a new role model, the new role model is likely to be just as busy as the old one.

Constant loneliness doesn't have to be a

### Activities for the Two of You

Preteens are ready for action and agile enough to enjoy sports that once frustrated them. At this age, kids are still willing to be seen with you in public, so enjoy these activities with them:

- Active sports. Plan a bike ride to a park or try your local bike trail. In winter, go cross-country skiing. These sports not only let kids work off excess energy, but they also give you a chance to talk.
- Spectator sports. Preteens' strong sense of loyalty is especially fun when they're cheering for a local team. You'll find everything from soccer to gymnastics at the high school in your area. Find out which sports intrigue your child and make a habit of attending the events.
- Board and card games. Kids of this age enjoy the competition and still get a kick out of beating you. Keep a supply of board games on hand for quiet times.
- Gardening. Preteens have the strength to dig and the tenacity to work side by side with you. Let your preteen plan the garden. Make an outing of buying seeds and tools. Set a regular time when you can tend the garden together. No yard? Try growing flowers or herbs indoors.

## Discipline Tip: Natural and Logical Consequences

Because preteens have such improved thinking skills, they respond to a logical approach to discipline. By this age, they see the connection between behavior and consequences. As a result, natural and logical consequences can reduce their misbehavior.

Natural consequences occur if you do nothing to intervene. All kids learn from natural consequences, and the technique is very effective for kids who like power struggles or getting even with you. If you haven't intervened, your child can hardly blame you for the consequence.

Here are a few sample behaviors and their natural consequences:

| **Behavior** | **Natural Consequence** |
|---|---|
| Staying up too late | Being tired the next day |
| Leaving clothes in a heap | Having wrinkled clothes |
| Spending a lot of money on candy | Having no money to go to the movies |

But natural consequences aren't always feasible. Sometimes a behavior has no natural consequence, and other times, the natural consequence is dangerous or too long in coming to make an impact.

In those cases, it's better to use a logical consequence. A logical consequence is one you make up that teaches your child the give-and-take rules of society. Logical consequences should be tied to the misbehavior in two ways. First, they should be related in content: A child who spills her milk must wipe it up. This is related in content because she wipes up milk instead of losing her allowance or washing the toilet.

Second, the logical consequence should be tied to the behavior in intensity. If a child spills milk, she wipes the spot, but does not wash the entire floor. When your kids see that the logical consequence is related to misbehavior, they are more likely to think the consequence makes sense.

Here are some examples of misbehavior and their logical consequences:

| **Behavior** | **Logical Consequence** |
|---|---|
| Missing the bus | Walking to school |
| Coming home 20 minutes late | Coming home 20 minutes early the next day |
| Refusing to wear an apron | Not being allowed to cook |

To use logical consequences with your child, follow these steps:

1) Give the child a choice. ("You have a choice. You can put your bike away or not get to ride it next time.")
2) When you give the child a choice, do it in a firm but friendly tone. You're not trying to get revenge.
3) If your child still misbehaves, apply the consequence immediately, without a second warning. Tell your child that there will be a chance to try again later.
4) If your child repeats the behavior, repeat the choice and the consequence. Wait for a longer while before providing a chance to try again.

# Your 8- to 12-Year-Old

fact of life for preteens. A regular date to have lunch or go shopping alone with you helps stave off the child's feeling of being abandoned. A ritual good-night conversation one-on-one also can restore your preteen's feeling of being loved.

You may find that an after-school child-care program satisfies your child's dual need for friends and supervision. If that isn't possible, consider setting up a network of friends and neighbors your child can call or visit. An adult role model can be a source of companionship, too.

Preteens also may enjoy organized after-school activities. The band, the 4-H Club, or the soccer team will distract youngsters, give them a new circle of friends, and boost their self-esteem.

## Excessive Responsibility

Although some preteens feel overburdened by chores their parents have assigned, other youngsters assume responsibilities far beyond what anyone expects of them. After a divorce, some children go on a cleaning frenzy, for example, doing much more than their parents themselves would ever do. They regularly dust, vacuum, scour the sink, and wash the kitchen floor. They make dinner, set the table, and do the dishes. They keep their rooms spotless.

Many parents are delighted by their child's exaggerated sense of responsibility. How, they wonder, did they ever get so lucky?

Unfortunately, the news isn't all good. Preteens *can* contribute to the family and often feel stronger family ties when they do. But youngsters who shoulder too much responsibility miss out on something they can never replace—their childhood. Play is still an important part of growing up, even for pseudosophisticated preteens. Youngsters who don't develop social skills at this age will feel even more awkward when they reach adolescence.

Excessive responsibility not only interferes with childhood, it also masks the child's deep-seated fears. Kids who take on too many duties may do so because they are desperately afraid of losing their custodial parent. "If I keep the house clean, Dad will stay," they reason. "If I make dinner, Mom will still love me."

If your preteens are taking on too many chores, redirect their energies. Realize that you may have encouraged this behavior, and act less enthused when they clean up. Catch yourself before you praise them for dusting, and instead praise them for earning a scouting badge or for being the fastest runner on the block. Discuss the problem with your kids and enroll them in such activities as team swimming or drama lessons. Once they get involved, they won't have time to be such meticulous housekeepers, and their self-esteem will get a boost.

### Books for Your Preteen

*Boys' and Girls' Book About Divorce, The.* Gardner, Richard A. New York: Bantam Books, 1970.

*Dear Mr. Henshaw.* Cleary, Beverly. New York: Morrow, 1983.

*Divorce Express.* Danziger, Paula. New York: Delacorte, 1982.

*It's Not the End of the World.* Blume, Judy. New York: Dell, 1972.

*Kids' Book of Divorce, The: By, For and About Kids.* Rofes, Eric. Lexington, Mass.: Lewis Publishing Co., 1981.

*Mitzi's Honeymoon with Nana Potts.* Williams, Barbara. New York: E.P. Dutton, 1983.

*Mom Is Dating Weird Wayne.* Auch, Mary Jane. New York: Holiday House, 1988.

*My Mother Is Not Married to My Father.* Okomoto, Jean Davies. New York: Pocket Books, 1979.

*What's Going to Happen to Me?* Le Shan, Eda. Bristol, Fla.: Four Winds, 1978.

AS YOUR CHILD GROWS

# Your Teen

Trying to establish their own identities, teens waver between bravado and self-doubt. One day they're remarkably responsible; the next day, they're totally rebellious. This time can be exasperating for parents, but most teens emerge from adolescence with a renewed sense of self-esteem and become mature, considerate adults.

Adolescence is difficult enough for kids whose families are intact. But when parents divorce, the normal route of teen development is upset. Suddenly, teens who are supposed to be rebelling against their parents find that one parent isn't around much to rebel against. It's confusing for teens whose parents always played by the rules to find that those parents have broken some of the rules themselves. Divorce may create chaos when combined with the swirl of emotions teens already face as part of their normal course of development. Tempestuous reactions are normal as teens face the loss of the family they've known for years.

Although their reactions may be more intense, adolescents also have more resources than their younger siblings do. Teens' interests and friends act as a buffer against the pain the family experiences. Most teens also realize that they didn't cause the divorce, so they don't feel the guilt that plagues younger kids. And because teens are planning college and careers, they can imagine a day when they will leave home and put the pain behind them.

All teens experiment with language, music, and attitudes in an effort to establish their own identities. Their hairstyles, clothes, and beliefs can bewilder parents. But wise parents realize how innocuous most fads are and allow their teens wide latitude in choosing their own styles.

Your child's taste in clothing may seem bizarre, and you may wonder how a Democrat could emerge from Republican parents. For teens of divorce, the rebellion serves a dual purpose: Not only does it allow them to establish themselves as separate beings in the family, but it also lets them express anger in a harmless way. A few years of loud rock music and peculiar hairstyles are a small price to pay; the alternative is the reckless behavior adolescents try when they can't resolve their anger in another way.

## Withdrawal

Most teens spend a great deal of time alone in their rooms, looking for a refuge from the emotional storm that envelops them. For teens of divorce, the need for solitude may seem even more acute.

In an effort to blunt the pain of divorce, many adolescents distance themselves from the family. Some teens withdraw by giving only superficial answers to questions and volunteering no information. Others withdraw physically, going to their rooms or out of the house, in an attempt to escape the memories of happier times. Even teens in intact homes may avoid family functions because they are embarrassed at being seen with their parents. Teens in families of divorce also withdraw from family outings because the outings arouse so much pain.

Despite their claims to the contrary, teens need the support of their family. Your teens need some time alone and some independence, but excessive or prolonged withdrawal should be considered a danger signal.

Many teens are rather blunt about their need for privacy. Their "Leave me alone!" shouts sting the parent who has tried to stay close. To a divorced parent, this feels like one more rejection. But patience in the face of your teens' withdrawal is a better course than withdrawing yourself. You may need to ignore their initial protests; many teens who tell you to get off their back will spill everything if you just stick with them quietly for a few minutes.

Some divorced parents also find withdrawal difficult to accept because they are lonely and miss their child's companionship. Your teens can empathize with this loneliness. By explaining your

# Your Teen

feelings you can help your adolescents understand why their withdrawal bothers you. Telling them, "I miss the time we used to spend together," can put the situation in a whole new light. Without this explanation, most teens view your requests for time together as mere meddling.

However, no teen should be expected to satisfy your needs for company. It's tempting to make your teen your best friend, but the match won't satisfy either of you in the end. If you pursue your own activities and friendships, you'll provide your teen with a far better model, and each of you will be more interesting to the other.

## Lack of Motivation

Some adolescents react to divorce with what looks like total apathy. They lose interest in friends and family. Their grades slip and they do their homework halfheartedly. Jobs and activities that once seemed to be a real source of pride now hold little interest.

Lack of motivation is related to the teen's self-esteem. Most children feel unloved after a divorce. Even teens who understand that they didn't cause the divorce might think, "If Dad loved me, he would have stayed. But he left, so I must not be lovable."

Adolescents may berate themselves endlessly; not only do they feel unloved, but they also feel they will never amount to much. They expect to fail in school, at work, and with friends. If they're going to fail anyway, they reason, why bother trying in the first place?

Most teens also are very angry about divorce. Instead of expressing anger through normal adolescent rebellion, some teens go on strike. They try to get back at their parents by refusing to do anything. Others turn their anger inward and find that repressing anger takes all their energy. As a result, they have no strength left for chores, schoolwork, or friends.

Noncustodial parents can reawaken adolescents' motivation by proving that they still care. Frequent phone calls and visitations, even when the teen seems sullen or angry, will assure your youngsters that both parents intend to play an active, interested role in their lives.

An apathetic teen also may be imitating a depressed parent. If your teens see you staying home from work, losing interest in other activities, or letting your appearance deteriorate, they may follow your example. If you are concerned about your teen's lack of interest, consider your own state of mind. Counseling may help both of you.

### Distress Signals

It's not easy to sort out the normal turmoil of adolescence from real danger signs. It's tempting to deny problems exist by sloughing them off as a phase your kid is going through.

But because teens try everything once and think nothing bad will ever happen to them, you're smart to be wary. Symptoms overlap, so leave the diagnosis to a professional. Any of these signs could indicate trouble; get immediate help if you see several signs at once.

Distress signals include:

- Truancy, tardiness, or falling grades
- Sudden change in friends
- Impulsive behavior
- Unexplained injuries
- Perpetual conflict with others
- Marked weight gain or loss
- Frequent sleeping problems
- Talking about suicide or hurting oneself, even in a joking way
- New possessions you can't afford
- Problems with the law
- Giving away possessions
- Consistent curfew violations
- Loss of job
- Drug-related paraphernalia
- Clothes that bear gang symbols or drug slogans
- Unusually influential friends
- Discussion of satanic rituals

## Recklessness

Trying to break away from the family isn't easy for any teen. It's hard to test a family's values, yet that is exactly what teens need to do in order to establish their own identities and define their beliefs.

All teens need to rebel against something, so don't worry if your once-compliant child becomes unruly in adolescence. However, teens whose parents have divorced may not have much structure to rebel against. A teen from an intact home may rebel by staying out after curfew; a teen whose parent is too exhausted to enforce curfew will flail around and look for other ways to rebel.

These teens may find dangerous ways of getting in trouble. The devil-may-care attitude of the teen years can lead any teen to experiment with drugs, sex, and crime, but for children of divorce, these escapes are particularly appealing. Some teens try to blot out problems in a haze of alcohol and sex; others become reckless to express their anger and get your attention.

Recklessness can have long-lasting effects. Many teens in distress can't stop with a few experiments with drugs, but instead become habitual users. Like other teens, they consider themselves invincible, never imagining that drug abuse can have serious consequences.

Teens who feel rejected at home may try to win acceptance through their peer group—even if that involves risky ventures. Looking for love, they become promiscuous. This is especially true for girls, even girls whose parents divorced long ago. Some become promiscuous as a way of competing

### Discipline Tip: Conflict Resolution

Teens hate to be treated like little kids and resent rules that seem arbitrary. If you say, "Do it because I told you to," they'll dig in their heels and flatly refuse to obey.

Instead of issuing edicts, take advantage of your teens' ability to reason by using conflict resolution. By involving them in this process of problem-solving, you acknowledge their power and put it to good use. To use conflict resolution:

1) In a quiet moment, identify the problem. Use the word "I" instead of "you" to show how you feel. For instance: "I'm tired of finding an empty refrigerator when I'm hungry or want to offer food to our guests. What can we do to solve this problem?"

2) Brainstorm solutions. Get your child to offer as many ideas as possible. Don't judge the ideas yet; just list them on paper. Here's how the list might look for the problem above:

a) Mom will put a sticker on packages of food she is saving for company.

b) If I eat the last of anything, I'll replace it before she gets home.

c) I won't do any snacking.

d) When we're running out of something, we will add it to the grocery list on the refrigerator door.

e) Mom won't buy food for guests until the last possible minute.

3) Evaluate the ideas together. Narrow down your list to the ideas that will work best for you. You might decide that example "e" won't work for you, while your child throws out example "c."

4) Decide how to put the ideas to use. Ask, "Do we need anything to start this? Who's doing what? When do we start?" In this case, you'd need stickers and a grocery list.

5) After you've tried the plan for a while, re-evaluate. If it's not working for one of you, try the process again.

# Your Teen

with their parents, who may be dating other people again. Others become promiscuous because it makes them feel like adults.

Promiscuity can be a real danger. Despite sex education classes, most teens don't look beyond the moment. Because they ignore long-term consequences, they take no precautions to ensure safe sex. Pregnancy and sexually transmitted diseases are real possibilities.

Shortsightedness can have other consequences as well. Teens from divorced families are more likely to drop out of school. Some shoplift or steal cars with no thought of the consequences, much less any consideration of their victims. Others run away from home, never imagining how difficult it is to survive on the streets.

Reckless teens have an "I'll show you" attitude and a desperate need to prove how adult they are. Yet, most of them long for the sweet days of childhood. They will feel far more secure if you let them recall those memories of an intact family. You may not want your ex-spouse's belongings around, but your son may be comforted by his dad's baseball cap. Your daughter may need to pore over photo albums, remembering times when her mom was still around. Those memories reassure her that she was loved by both parents.

You also can reassure your teens by enforcing reasonable rules. Despite their rebellion, adolescents need and want limits. Having no limits or limits that aren't enforced makes teens very anxious. To relieve that anxiety, they'll try anything, just to get a reaction. It may seem to take all your energy to enforce household rules, but it's worth the effort. Your consistency will reassure them, and they'll feel more settled at home.

Many teens also thrive on activity. They can plunge wholeheartedly into sports, band, school plays, and the yearbook. Some teens like the independence they get from having a job (limited to fewer than 20 hours per week). Volunteer work keeps teens busy and lets them test out careers.

If your teen does develop reckless behavior, take immediate action. Ask the teachers if they have observed the same

## Activities for the Two of You

Suddenly you're caught in the push-pull of adolescence. When friends visit, your teen shoves you away, embarrassed by your presence. Yet the same kid talks for hours when you're alone. In fact, many parents find that divorce brings them much closer to their teens. Tap into that closeness with these activities:

- Go out to eat. Teens love the sophistication and enjoy conversation. Breakfast together can start the whole day on a bright note. Dinner with you can make up for many lonely times. Teens love experiments, so try that ethnic café that intrigues you.
- See a play. Teens are naturally dramatic and love theater. You don't need a professional performance; high schools, colleges, and community groups all offer inexpensive shows. Can't afford a ticket? Offer to be an usher and you'll see the show free.
- Cook. Make pizza, pancakes, or cookies. There's nothing like an hour in the kitchen gabbing to bring you closer together. And there's nothing like sharing the results to bring on a satisfied sigh (or a giggle, if you have a disaster).
- Do volunteer work. Teens love to immerse themselves in causes and can work tirelessly for goals they believe in. The shared experience of selling candy or passing water to thirsty runners will make you feel doubly good: You'll be proud of your child and happy to be helping others.

symptoms. Today, adolescents are fortunate to have an array of support systems, from self-help groups for drug abuse to residential treatment for disturbed youngsters. A doctor, counselor, or social worker can put you in touch with appropriate services. The sooner you take action, the more likely your adolescent is to recover.

## Assigning Blame

Adolescents are romantic by nature, expecting all relationships to work like fairy tales. As a result, they find your divorce unnerving. It makes them wonder whether divorce runs in families and whether they'll ever be able to maintain a stable relationship themselves.

Many young adolescents also cling to rather black-and-white views of morality and feel that one of the parents must have been entirely at fault in the divorce. Holding just one person responsible allows them to whitewash the other. And since young teens long for idols, they assign this role to the "blameless" parent.

Blaming just one parent also gives adolescents one person who spells "safety." If they can blame Dad for everything, then living with Mom will be more comfortable. If they can blame Mom for everything, even if they live with her, there's always the hope that life with Dad would be paradise.

It's tempting to contribute to your child's sense of blame by criticizing your ex-spouse and reveling in the saintly image your teen may bestow upon you. In fact, you may be contributing to that behavior by holding yourself up as nearly perfect.

Pretending to be a saint while criticizing your ex-spouse can backfire in two ways. You set yourself up as an unreachable model for your children, who feel that they can never measure up to your standards. And later in adolescence, when your teens discover your imperfections, they will feel betrayed and bitter.

Even if you don't criticize your ex-spouse, though, your teen may come to the conclusion that the ex-spouse is entirely to blame. It's simply a more comfortable notion for youngsters at this age.

Sometimes one parent really is to blame, as in the case of abandonment. In such cases, tell your teens what happened without glossing over the situation.

There also are circumstances in which blame will be less of an issue. If your spouse was mentally ill and did not succeed in controlling the illness, teens will be relieved to know that their parent did not leave the family due to a lack of love, but due to a problem that is hard to control.

To help your child, explain that in any conflict, two people usually are at fault. The reasons you gave for the divorce can provide a starting point for discussion. For instance, teens who've been told that you and your ex-spouse just grew apart can understand that as they outgrow old friends and make new ones.

No matter what the situation, most teens need to learn that blame isn't very useful. They may be angry, but they can find many more constructive ways to express anger than taking it out on a parent.

### Books for Your Teen

*Leap Before You Look.* Stolz, Mary. New York: Harper and Row, 1972.

*Moonlight Man, The.* Fox, Paula. New York: Dell, 1988.

*Open Mind, An.* Sallis, Susan. New York: Harper and Row, 1978.

*Stepkids: A Survival Guide for Teenagers in Stepfamilies.* Getzoff, Ann, and McClenahan, Carolyn. New York: Walker and Co., 1984.

*Tangle of Roots, A.* Girion, Barbara. New York: Putnam, 1985.

CAT

# LIFE AFTER DIVORCE

With divorce comes a complete change in lifestyle. Noncustodial parents may feel lost living alone. Custodial parents may stagger under the burden of making decisions alone. It feels strange to make an appointment to see your kids, and it feels equally strange to give them up on schedule. Many parents also experience a dramatic change in their standard of living.

Yet, while you rebuild your life, the children can hardly be put on hold. They still have needs and long for your support in the family crisis. Dealing with their needs as well as custody, visitation, and finances takes a good deal of juggling, patience, and communication.

## Communicating with Your Ex-Spouse

Poor communication between parents creates many problems for children of divorce. It isn't easy to communicate with someone who reminds you of a painful past, but for your children's well-being, it's essential to communicate regularly with your ex-spouse.

To keep communication neutral, think of your child's needs and of your communication as a way to meet those needs. By keeping your child's needs in mind, it will be easier to be civil with your ex-spouse.

In the first few months after divorce, it may be too painful to talk with your ex-spouse. Use the mail for messages until you feel stronger. (If you need to use the mail for more than a few months, see a therapist.)

Most people prefer communication that's direct and scheduled at a time and place that are convenient for both parties. Schedule calls or meetings in advance for a limited period of time when the two of you are relaxed.

A neutral turf also helps some couples remain civil. Meeting in a restaurant may be more conducive to quiet, polite talk than meeting at home. When you do get together, remember to set a limited goal for the meeting: making plans for the kids' summer vacation, for instance. With the goal in mind, you can focus the discussion toward the children's needs.

Using "I messages" also helps. Instead of using the word "you," take responsibility for your feelings. Rather than saying, "You never did respect my job; you always stood in the way," say, "I feel anxious when you're late for lunch because I have a limited lunch hour and can't be late." Starting with "I feel" helps you communicate honestly without attacking your ex-spouse.

But even careful communication can arouse strong feelings. If you sense an argument building, stop. Take a break and try again when you feel ready. The break may be a trip to the rest room or a cooling-off period of several days, but it will be more constructive than shouting.

To prevent problems, stay in touch. Keep your ex-spouse informed. If you are the custodial parent, urge the children to share their schoolwork with your ex-spouse. Be sure to notify your ex-spouse of school functions and Little League games.

If special needs arise, or if you'd like to make a change in plans, ask your ex-spouse instead of assuming that the answer will be no. Many noncustodial parents will gladly rearrange visitation so the kids can go camping. But they can't read your mind.

**Avoiding undermining.** Your feelings about your ex-spouse and your children's feelings will differ. They may still love someone you now despise, because they had different experiences as children than you had as a spouse. Most children will want to maintain their relationship with the other parent—even with a parent who seems intolerable to you.

Try to communicate as fairly about your ex-spouse as you did about the divorce. You may feel angry, hurt, and bitter. But if you relay these feelings to the children, they may develop lasting problems. For their sake, vent your feelings out of the kids' earshot. See a therapist, join a support group, ask your ex-spouse to call when the kids are asleep, or all of the above.

Of course, you can't avoid all mention of your ex-spouse. However, you can avoid certain expressions. You may need a cue, such as a sign in the kitchen or a ring, that will remind you to avoid any of the following kinds of phrases.

"If he really cared about you, he'd make the child support payments on time."

"You're as sloppy as your mother was."

"If he's late picking you up again, I'm not going to let him see you."

"Surely you don't believe your mother when she says that, do you?"

"We'd still be together today if it hadn't been for you."

Instead of saying something you'll regret, practice saying these kinds of phrases:

"I know you miss your mother terribly."

"That's something you need to discuss with your father; I can't answer it."

"We loved each other very much and that's why we had you. Even though we got a divorce, we'll both always love you."

"It's OK to be angry; you can be angry with your mother but still love her."

"Have you asked your dad for that? It can't hurt to ask."

**If you are being undermined.** Some parents are determined to support the ex-spouse, only to find that the other parent is undermining them. If you want to cooperate with your ex-spouse, but find that he or she is eroding your authority, you must confront your ex-spouse directly. Your friends, relatives, and counselor can support you, but they can't do this for you.

When you meet with your ex-spouse, explain how you feel about being undermined, how it affects the children, and what you would like changed. Also let your ex-spouse know that you don't intend to retaliate.

For example, you might say, "When I pick the children up, they are at their worst behavior. They mock me, talk back, and refuse to obey. I've heard them talk with you on the phone, and it sounds as if you're encouraging them to make fun of me. We may not get along as a couple any more, but we are both still their parents, and I can't enforce rules if you cut me down behind my back. I support you in your decisions with them, and I expect the same from you."

In most cases, direct confrontation will be enough. But if the problem continues, meet with the entire family. In front of the children, ask the other parent to stop, and ask the kids not to erode your authority, even if the other parent tempts them to do so. Tell the children that you don't undermine the other parent and that you expect them not to undermine you.

Some parents find it useful to have a counselor or mediator present when they confront the ex-spouse. Others draw up a written agreement with the other parent, spelling out exactly what each parent will do to respect the other's authority.

## Custody

Although at one time the courts automatically awarded custody to the divorced mother, that pattern has been changing. Parents are becoming quite creative in the arrangements they work out.

Sometimes the least traditional arrangements work better than you would have imagined. Even if your ex-spouse was a terrible parent before the divorce, the pattern can change. Some people become better parents after a divorce than they were before because they can focus on the children in a way they never could during the stress of a deteriorating marriage.

In most cases, the mother still becomes the primary caregiver after divorce. This practice is based partly on tradition and partly on the fact that relatively few fathers seek primary custody. Many women also feel pressured to seek custody because they think there is a social bias against mothers who give up custody.

If the mother had assumed most of the child-care responsibilities, placing children with the mother may seem to be the obvious choice. You may reach that conclusion because you think the mother would have fewer adjustments to make than the father.

However, this isn't always the case. Some mothers who are thrust into the work force for the first time, or who must re-enter the work force after many years, find the combination of full-time work and parenting too much. Some fathers become better caregivers after divorce, leaping into the custodial role where they used to linger in the background, deferring to their wives.

For some fathers, winning custody is wonderful. They can nurture their children without feeling intimidated by the sex-role definitions of years past. For other fathers, the image of one big happy family dissolves in a dizzying round of diapers, day-care problems, and discipline matters. Fathers assuming child-care responsibilities for the first time may feel overwhelmed.

Joint custody is another option that helps both parents remain active in the children's lives. Because the concept of joint custody has varied so widely, states are trying to clarify the term. In most places, joint custody now means that both parents share major decisions about the kids. They must come to agreement on education, religious training, and health care. They may attend parent conferences together and meet at the doctor's office when their child is ill.

Joint custody can mean joint physical custody, but it doesn't have to. Parents have devised some ingenious arrangements for sharing physical custody, with the children spending varying amounts of time with each parent.

Some families use a split-week arrangement. The children live with the father for one half of the week, and with the mother for the other. Another plan is the alternating-week arrangement, where the kids spend one week with the father and the next with the mother. Both plans work best when parents live near one another so the children can attend the same school all the time. These plans take a great deal of coordination and communication, but many children find it less painful to leave one parent when they expect to see that parent again in just a few days.

Other parents use an alternate-year plan, where the children spend one year with the mother and the next year with the father. If you use this plan, be sure the kids see your ex-spouse often. This plan doesn't take quite as much coordination as the split-week approach, but it may be harder on you and the children.

Another approach is the shared-home plan, in which the kids stay home and the parents switch houses every week. Originally, many judges thought this would be the best approach for joint custody, because children would not have the stress of moving between two homes. But many families who started using this approach found it unworkable and eventually switched to another plan. Some kids find it

## Rethinking Custody Decisions

Even the best custody plans may have to change over time. Your needs, the needs of your ex-spouse, and the needs of your children will evolve over the years, and a change in custody may be beneficial.

Some noncustodial parents go to court to seek custody with good intentions, never realizing that their urge to have the children may not have a solid footing. Ask yourself these questions before you ask for custody:

- Do you just want to see the kids more often? Most judges would gladly award you more time. In fact, you may not need a judge at all; you can arrange this on your own or use a mediator.
- Are you lonely? Expand your circle of friends instead of asking your children to ease the loneliness.
- Are you seeking custody because you are feeling guilty? Explore your feelings with a therapist.
- Are you being pressured into custody by someone else or by your own need for revenge? If your friends are all seeking custody, you may feel the need to do so, too. Remember, you'll have to bear the responsibilities that come with custody.
- How would your life change if the children were with you? Consider the changes you'd have to make in your lifestyle, social life, and career goals. Can you make those changes?
- When the kids say they want to live with you, do they really just mean they you? Many parents are overjoyed when a child asks to live with them. Your child may associate the phrase "I want to live with you" with affection.
- Are the children accusing the other parent of neglect or abuse? They may be retaliating for the custodial parent's strict rules, or they may be telling the truth. Ask a doctor or therapist to evaluate any complaints the children have.
- Is your child trying to avoid something at the other home? Perhaps your son hopes that by moving in with you, he will have to change schools and get away from his math teacher.
- Are the children unrealistic about living with you? They may think that life with you would be one big party.
- Will you and the kids be happy? If you have to make drastic changes, either by uprooting the kids from friends and school, or by dramatically altering your own life, custody may not be for you.

confusing to have two sets of rules and traditions in the same home. In essence, although everyone lives at the house, it doesn't seem like anyone's home.

When you and your ex-spouse cannot agree about custody, the judge may have to decide. This is a lengthy, costly, and exhausting process that holds no guarantees. Consult a mediator first. Custody plans worked out together usually are more satisfying and allow change as family circumstances change.

Whether you go to court or not, you may be tempted to have the kids decide the custody issue. But for some children, the choice is painful. They are being asked to choose between two people they love, and choosing one over the other makes children feel disloyal. The younger the children are, the more painful the decision is for them. Don't put young children in that position. Your teens may handle the matter well, but even they may dread being asked. It is usually an adult decision.

## Visitation

The visitation you and your spouse work out will make a big difference in the children's adjustment. You can make visitation work by remembering that children need both parents and by keeping the schedule and environment stable. Make the visits predictable. Kids adjust far better if they know exactly when they will see their other parent. For young children, a calendar with color-coded visitation days helps reduce the anxiety aroused by abstract promises such as "Daddy will come to see you on Saturday."

Kids also feel better if they know they'll see the other parent again soon. Short visits with short breaks between visits are preferable to long visits with long breaks in between. Long breaks make each separation more painful. Also, it's easier for children to forget the routines in each house when the time between visits is long. Their behavior deteriorates because they simply can't recall the rules in each place.

To get the best behavior from kids, keep the rules in each home consistent. That doesn't mean that you and your ex-spouse must establish the same rules, although it's wonderful when you can. It does mean that in your own home, you adhere to the same rules and routines each time the children come. Kids can adapt to a 7:30 bedtime at their mother's and an 8:30 bedtime at their father's, but it's hard to adapt if the bedtime in each house always fluctuates.

Keep the physical surroundings consistent, too. Noncustodial parents can help the kids feel welcome by making sure that each child has a spot to call home, even if it's just a special place for the suitcase and a special chair in the living room. You might also urge the child to bring something familiar on every visit. A teddy bear, favorite storybook, or even a pillow can be a great source of continuity for your child.

Many noncustodial parents fall into the trap of putting on a show for their children during each visitation. They visit every tourist spot for miles around, stuff the kids with delicious treats, and rack up purchases of toys and clothing. Children may enjoy this treatment initially, but they soon begin to view it as a bribe, whether the parent intends it that way or not.

### Grandparent Visitation

Grandparents may shudder at the thought of your divorce, even when they support your decision. The reason? Too often, divorce means that one set of grandparents will never see their grandchildren again.

But more and more grandparents are speaking up. Some find the matter easily resolved, because they already had a good relationship with their son- or daughter-in-law. They visit the grandchildren on a regular basis, alone. That preserves their role as grandparents and allows the kids to enjoy them without worrying about loyalty to either parent.

Most parents recognize that grandparents don't want to be divorced from grandchildren. However, if you are uncomfortable with your former in-laws visiting the kids alone, schedule a time when you, the children, and the grandparents can visit together. A Sunday dinner or walk in the park can be a relaxing time for everyone. It also helps you ensure that grandparents enforce the same rules you maintain.

## Visitation as Your Child Grows

Visitation should occur on an established schedule, but it need not be written in stone. Although frequent changes upset kids, some adaptation over time is needed to accommodate the needs of growing children.

Possible schedules are limited only by your child's needs and your own creativity. Here are a few visitation plans for children of different ages.

- For infants. Most babies do best when they stay home and the parents do the visiting. This eliminates the cumbersome transfer of diapers, cribs, and playpens from one house to another and gives the infant the security of a familiar place.
- For toddlers. Toddlers shouldn't be separated from primary caretakers for long. Some can handle an overnight stay with the noncustodial parent every few days. Phone calls from the noncustodial parent once or twice between visits will be reassuring.
- For children ages 4 to 12. By this age, children can handle longer visits. Split-week arrangements are possible for children older than 5 and work especially well if both parents live in the same school district.
- For adolescents. Teens need a same-sex role model, but they also want time with friends and balk at visiting every weekend. That's no reflection on the noncustodial parent; even the custodial parent sees less of kids this age. Teens need a say in the visitation schedule. They can tolerate longer stays and longer breaks between visits. They enjoy summers with one parent if they already have friends in that parent's neighborhood.

In fact, although your children don't want to be bored at your house, they also don't want to be treated like company. They'll feel more at ease if you create a typical home atmosphere when they visit. If they see you on weekends, think back to what you did on weekends before the divorce. You might have gone to the museum, but you also had errands to run. Kids long for the pleasure of your company. They'll gladly tag along to the library, the hardware store, and the post office, just to spend time with you.

That doesn't mean you should abandon all fun activities; it does mean that you can blend normal activities with special ones and maintain the relationship you've always enjoyed with the kids. When you bring them along on errands, they get a sense of contributing to your welfare, and you get the chores done without rushing to do everything before the kids come each week.

Between visitations, keep communication low-key but frequent. Even if you call the children every Sunday, they need to know they can call you anytime. You also can let them know you're accessible through other types of communication. You might give the kids self-addressed postcards to send you. Or record monologues on tape for them and invite them to do the same. No matter what method you choose, those frequent contacts will keep you in touch. In a weekend visit, kids don't always remember to tell you the little things that happen. But the little things make a big difference to them and to their relationship with you.

## Financial Arrangements

For many families, the emotional trauma of divorce is matched only by the financial one. Child support payments come late or not at all. Noncustodial parents wonder if the kids are really getting any of the child support money. And even a carefully planned settlement may cause problems later as children's needs change or parents switch jobs.

Therefore, consider the settlement temporary. That cooperative attitude can keep changes in financial arrangements from becoming an endless battle. For most people, this is preferable to legal fees and the agony of having every detail aired in public. Mediators can work out plans that are beneficial to parents and children. For instance, they may tie the child's standard of living to a percentage of the wealthier parent's income, no matter who is wealthier at the time. As parents change jobs, the support amount changes, too.

Even with the best of arrangements, divorce may bring a drastic change in your standard of living. Children may find such financial changes difficult to understand. Some children move from a spacious home in the suburbs to a cramped apartment on a dirty city street. Others find that their requests for spending money are met with a new refrain, "I'm sorry, but we just can't afford it."

As a rule, kids are better off understanding the general financial status of the household. If money is tight, tell the children. They don't have to know every detail, but they will be more reasonable in their requests if they know what to expect.

You may think the kids have suffered enough and shouldn't have money problems on top of everything else. Perhaps you're inclined to buy them everything they want, even if you must go without. But if you sacrifice everything for them, you may harbor resentment. And once they find out you've been so self-sacrificing, they may feel guilty and angry.

Despite the government's increased efforts at enforcing child support payments, your ex-spouse may be delinquent with payments. That may tempt you to withhold visitation rights. However, few judges would uphold that practice. Besides, you run the risk of alienating your children.

Instead, act quickly the first time your ex-spouse defaults, before the amount missing becomes overwhelming. Contact your state's Child Support Enforcement Administration, the National Council for Children's Rights, or the Association for Children for Enforcement of Support. Write for the Handbook on Child Support Enforcement (see pages 62-63).

If you are the noncustodial parent, you may feel that you must pay without having any say in how the kids are raised. Or you may dislike sending payments to your ex-spouse and think the children should know where the money is coming from. Some noncustodial parents send a check made out to the child, who gleefully spends it on extras, leaving nothing for such essentials as groceries. But the fact is that the noncustodial parent can't control the way the money is spent. If you suspect that your ex-spouse is living high on your child support, then renegotiate the payments.

One alternative is to tell your teens what you contribute. You also can ask the custodial parent to give you credit for contributing, perhaps by mentioning that "Mom sent money for your piano lessons" or "I really appreciate the way your dad always sends us the checks on time."

Many parents find it helpful to get financial counseling to prepare for routine and unforeseen expenses. You might have a small amount of money deducted from each paycheck and deposited in an account that is earmarked for emergencies.

In addition, many noncustodial parents want to contribute to their child's college education. You might have the college bill you directly. Or you might set up a trust fund in your child's name. A financial counselor can assist you in planning for your child's future.

# DATING AND REMARRIAGE

As frightening as it may seem, dating after divorce can be an integral and positive part of your growth as an individual. It can be an exhilarating outlet and a way to pursue new interests and hobbies with someone else. The attention you give to someone new can take your mind off your role as parent, and the attention you receive in return can be a boost to your self-esteem.

Dating does complicate life, however. Although you may be excited by the prospect of meeting someone new, your children probably won't share that excitement. In fact, most children are upset when a parent starts to date. Dating forces the children to accept the fact that their parents aren't going to remarry one another—and that's a painful process for most children.

Preteens and teens tend to be most upset by their parents' dating. They are independent enough to disagree with you at times, but they are not mature enough to adjust to your new life as quickly and enthusiastically as you will. Uncomfortable with their own emerging sexuality, teens and preteens find your dating unsettling. Each time you date, they realize that you are a sexual being, and that reminds them of their own sexual insecurity. These youngsters may be very outspoken, bluntly telling you why you shouldn't date.

Many children also conclude that dating leads to remarriage, and they fear that if you get remarried, you will desert them. Instead of expressing that fear, however, some youngsters sabotage the relationship. They may embarrass you, "forget" to relay phone messages, or act rudely toward your date.

However, not all children are upset when a parent dates. Some children view every date as a potential new parent—a parent they've been dreaming of. These youngsters may go out of their way to please your date, being overly affectionate or showing off their talents. They're terrified of rejection and worried that they may not be good enough for your date, so they compensate by being extra friendly.

Regardless of your children's views, you will probably date a number of people. It may be difficult on your children to see someone as a potential parent, only to find you dating someone new a few weeks later.

To spare your children the emotional ups and downs of the dating game, think of dating as only one part of your social life. If you make efforts to expand your circle of friends in general and invite a variety of people into your home, your children won't be as alarmed each time someone new enters their lives. Some parents accomplish this by joining an organization of single parents, such as Parents Without Partners. In fact, get-togethers that include the children can reduce the stress of trying to meet others, because you can always focus on the children. (That doesn't mean you should plan your entire social life around your children, though.)

It's also a good idea to wait before you introduce someone new to the children. Schedule your first few dates at a location away from home. That allows you to get to know each other without the added pressure of worrying about the children.

Once you've established a relationship, you can introduce that person to the

children. In fact, you should introduce anyone who has become important to you to the children. Your children will adjust to your new relationship far more readily if they have more time to get used to the idea.

Like all relationships, the children's relationship with anyone you date will need time and freedom to grow. As your date becomes more comfortable with the children, and vice versa, you can increase the amount of time you all spend together. By proceeding from simple conversations to watching a TV show as a group to going to the circus together, you'll ease your children and your date into friendship.

But don't expect your child to enjoy the company of your new friend if you've dragged everyone along on an outing meant for adults only. When you feel that the time is right, schedule an activity your child enjoys, and bring the child along on your date. If you plan carefully, your child will be more relaxed and able to enjoy the experience. As a result, so will you.

## The Question of Sex

As a relationship progresses, you may wonder about being affectionate: Will your children be upset if you hug or kiss in front of them? And will they be psychologically harmed if you bring someone home to spend the night?

Most parents find that a gradual approach works best. Just as you ease the children into accepting your relationship, you also can ease them into understanding that you are fond of your new friend and want to express that physically. Being cautious, you might avoid kissing and hugging in front of the children the first few times your friend visits the house. Although some children are upset by seeing you be affectionate with someone new, they won't be quite as upset if they have time to adjust to it.

The same approach can be used to answer the question of sleeping together. If your children were to see you bringing home someone different every night, the endless parade of visitors would confuse and frighten them. At the other extreme, if you sleep together but always hide it from the children, they will feel betrayed once they discover you. Besides, that kind of secrecy sends the wrong message to the children.

Each couple must make a decision about sleeping together based on their own beliefs. Some couples decide not to sleep together because they worry about the way their teens will react. Others decide to sleep together and answer the teen's "If you do it, why can't I?" by explaining the emotional and physical risks of sex and pregnancy for adolescents. Teens simply aren't mature enough to undertake something as serious as sharing their bodies with someone else.

Be aware that some children who rebel against your values in other ways may simply follow your example where sex is involved because they are eager to experiment at that age. Other kids hope that you will give them a reason to say "no" to peer pressure with your example.

If you do decide to sleep together, you can explain your decision fairly simply, without going into all the details. In other words, tell the truth, but not the whole truth. For instance, for young children, you might say, "Bob and I like each other very much. When a man and a woman like each other that much, they want to cuddle and sleep together. Bob is going to stay here tonight and sleep in my room."

You also can take steps to preserve your own privacy by hanging a "do not disturb" sign on the bedroom door. Make a habit of it long before anyone spends the night, just so that it becomes a routine the children grow to expect. That way, it won't come as a surprise to them to find a "do not disturb" sign on the door the first time someone stays overnight.

Use the same caution if you decide to live together. To explain the move, you might say, "You know that Michael and I really love each other. But I made a mistake once before when I married your father. I don't want to make a mistake like that again, so I want to be sure things will work out if I get married again. Michael is going to move in and live with us here so we can see whether we're good for each other."

Be sure that you are comfortable with the idea of living together before you take that step. And above all, don't expect your child to hide your new living arrangements from anyone. Asking your child not to tell anyone puts the youngster in a terrible position. Most children feel guilty that they have to lie and are ashamed of your relationship as a result. If you are ashamed of living together, your children will be, too.

If and when you end a long-term relationship, you should explain the breakup to the children. The pain you experience in ending the relationship will probably mirror the feelings you experienced during the divorce. Likewise, if your children have become attached to your friend, they will be distressed when the relationship ends. They may go through some of the same stages they experienced when you and your spouse separated. However, although the break up will be painful for them, the feelings won't be as lasting as those that followed the divorce.

Take your time in resolving any issues related to dating and sex. Children need time to adjust, and so do you. It's also wise to realize that your children still need you when you are in love; in fact, they may need you even more then because your new relationship threatens them. Set aside time to spend with them so they don't feel like castoffs as a result of the relationship. If you spend time with them, you won't be able to spend every waking minute with your new friend. That may be frustrating, but it will give the relationship a chance to grow. In the end, you, your friend, and your children will feel sure of one another and more comfortable.

## Preparing for Remarriage

The thought of remarriage can be exhilarating, frightening, and bewildering. Since you've already been through a divorce, you are probably more cautious about your second marriage. On the other hand, you probably feel more experienced and more certain of what you want.

Just as you proceeded slowly into dating, you'll be wise to move slowly into remarriage. Second marriages are more likely to fail than first marriages, and there are definite advantages to remaining single. As you contemplate remarriage, carefully examine your motives for remarrying.

Sometimes divorced people consider remarrying in order to provide a second parent for their children and make the family feel whole again. You may be dating someone who is very fond of your children, and very good with them, besides. But if you are only lukewarm about your own relationship as a couple, it won't matter how much your new partner loves your children. The marriage won't be satisfying, regardless of how good your parenting skills are.

If you decide to get married because of your love for each other, the relationship has a much better chance of succeeding. Still, remarriage isn't easy. You may be ecstatic; your children may not be.

When you remarry, your children must give up all their fantasies that you and your ex-spouse will get married to each other again. You may think, "Haven't we been through all this before?" Well, yes and no. You may have explained several times that you and your ex-spouse will not remarry each other. You may even have thought that by dating you put all your children's fantasies to rest. But some children won't give up those dreams until they absolutely have to.

Even when your children love your new spouse-to-be, they miss the old spouse. That's why your children may behave in unexpected ways when you announce your

engagement. The 5-year-old who always sat in your friend's lap may suddenly become belligerent. The 8-year-old who loved to get bear hugs may be distant and disobedient. And the adolescent who enjoyed your friend's banter and teasing may get sullen and moody.

Of course, you and your new spouse have some adjusting to do as well. Even if you lived together before marrying, you will find some reactions and habits in your new spouse that surprise you. But your children may have even more surprises. Not only do they have to get used to a new stepparent, but they also have to get used to a new you. As you become closer to your spouse-to-be, you may discard habits that the children considered family traditions. This puzzles them and may frighten them a bit because they long for the security that family routines can bring.

Children also find remarriage hard to accept because of their conflicting loyalties. They may have a new stepparent, but they still want to stay loyal to their old parent. They may also feel pressure from that other parent, who might act jealous, either cutting back on visitation and child support or becoming possessive and rigid about visitation schedules. Either way, the child will react.

Besides adjusting to you and your spouse-to-be, your children may have to adjust to a new house. The girl who grew up with a room of her own now may have to share a room with her stepsister. The boy who kept a hamster in his bedroom may suddenly find that it's living in the basement. And little ones who like to flock around the kitchen table may notice that you can't even fit a table in your new kitchen.

Family ranks may also change. An only child may suddenly have siblings. The oldest kid in your family may be only second or third in the new unit. Surrounded by strangers, any child may begin to feel like an outsider.

For adolescents, your marriage couldn't come at a worse time. The whole point of adolescence is to learn to pull away from the family and gradually establish a separate identity. When you remarry, you are asking your adolescent to do just the opposite—to become part of a new family. Expecting an adolescent to get close to stepparents is unrealistic and likely to backfire.

## Succeeding as A Stepfamily

How can you help your stepfamily succeed? First, by recognizing that the mere presence of a family stirs up painful memories for each member of the family. Each person recalls their original family unit with a combination of fond memories and regret. Every person in the household is still likely to feel part of a failed family, so their self-esteem won't be very high.

To cope with this stress, begin by taking care of yourself. Dress well, spend some time alone each day, and do something that makes you feel proud of yourself. Regular exercise can increase your energy level and improve your outlook. You might even schedule a time to exercise together with your spouse. Many couples find that bicycling or walking together gives them a chance to talk privately and cements their relationship.

You can help others in the family maintain their self-esteem, too. Just one positive comment a day can do wonders for a person's self-image. Admire your son's artistic talent, tell your stepdaughter how bright she is, and express your appreciation for your spouse. You may be pleasantly surprised to find that praise is contagious; the more often you praise others, the more you're likely to get praised in return.

By praising family members, you also open the door to building relationships. Be sure to spend time alone with your stepchildren, and allow your spouse to spend time alone with your children. But remember that those relationships won't grow overnight.

Teaching children a new skill or hobby also can establish a bond between stepparents and children. Most children are receptive to learning something new, even if they're initially reluctant to spend time with you. Teach them to play "Chopsticks," to grind coffee beans, or to do a cannonball dive. Don't insist on perfection or supervise them too closely; just approach it as if you expect the experience to be fun. Most children will enjoy watching you and then trying the skill themselves.

You also can tap into the children's appreciation of money as a way to strengthen family ties. Kids know that it takes money to raise a family, and they admire generosity. You can become generous in their eyes if you are the one to hand out allowances, treat them to an ice-cream cone, or buy them new jeans to replace a tattered pair. This doesn't mean that you should get on an endless round of gift-giving, but it does mean that you occasionally can act as provider.

One gift you can give to everyone is a new home. Each person in the family probably had a unique space in the house to call their own, and when families come together, it's easy to step on someone's territory. By moving into a new home, you're signaling to your spouse and children that this is a new life, a new start together, without the old patterns that were set in each household.

You may be worried that the children will get upset by this change, and they may indeed, but you can give them a sense of continuity by allowing them to keep their treasured bedspreads, bookshelves, and toy boxes. You also can help the children keep in touch with old friends by inviting children from the old neighborhood over to the new house.

Stepchildren also will adjust better if they think they can trust you. That means keeping your promises. If you've planned to take the family on a picnic on Saturday, don't put it off until Sunday. If you tell them you'd enjoy going miniature golfing, tell them when you plan to go—and don't cancel at the last minute. And if you promise to keep a secret, don't reveal it to anyone.

Above all, be honest with your stepchildren. Instead of quietly steaming inside, tell them when something bothers you. The most effective way is to use an "I message," focus on their behavior, and explain how it affects you: "When you tap your pencil, I get really annoyed," or "I can't hear the TV because the stereo is so loud," or "When you come home late and don't call first, I get worried about you." Explaining your feelings openly demonstrates your concern and helps the children view your request as concern instead of meddling.

## Putting Stepfamily Myths to Rest

*The Sound of Music. The Brady Bunch. Yours, Mine, and Ours.* Hollywood is full of warm, wonderful stories of blended families that worked. But unfortunately, these celluloid images are not realistic models for stepfamilies. In fact, if you set the von Trapp Family as your standard, you're heading for trouble. The von Trapp Family was the Hollywood version of stepfamily life—complete with sugarcoated problems and a happy ending.

You wouldn't model the rest of your life after a movie, and you shouldn't try to model your stepfamily after one. Most stepfamilies find that the road to becoming a real family is a long and rocky one. And the stepfamilies that have the most trouble are those that expect no bumps in the road along the way.

Even if you're familiar with some of the myths, you may find others that surprise you. You'll have more success in integrating your new family if you confront these seven stepfamily myths:

**Myth 1: Stepfamilies are just like biological families.** Fact: They're not. Everyone in a stepfamily has experienced some loss. They may have lost a spouse or parent. They've had to give up their original image of a perfect family that lived happily ever after. And even stepparents who have never been married before have had to

relinquish their dreams of what families should be—dreams that usually include their own biological children and a spouse who hasn't been married before.

Feelings of loss may surface again and again as your stepfamily comes together and celebrates family milestones, such as the birth of a child. Children may see the new child as one more person who will take you away from them. Clinging to your image of a storybook family will only make you and your children disappointed.

Instead, if you can begin to picture your stepfamily as an exciting new breed of family that doesn't have to follow the same rules as other families, you'll find it easier to accept the adjustments.

**Myth 2: All members of the stepfamily will adjust quickly.** Fact: That doesn't happen even in biological families, where parents have nine months to get used to the idea of a child. And it certainly doesn't happen in stepfamilies, where more people have more adjustments to make—and often, less time in which to do so.

Children who always ate breakfast before getting dressed may balk at their new family's tradition of getting dressed first. A stepfather who never had children before may be overwhelmed at how messy kids can be. A mother who anticipated having a new husband to share the load may feel as if there's even less time than there was before.

One way to help the family come together is by discussing problems at a family meeting, where each person's opinion is valued. Family meetings can help children and parents see that there is no one "right" or "wrong" way to establish routines in a stepfamily. As you work on problems together, you'll develop workable alternatives that help all family members feel they are building new traditions.

Another way to support stepfamily adjustment is by sharing the expectations each of you had for the family. It's easier to accept a stepdaughter's urgent need for an allowance if you realize that she expected the remarriage to ease the financial strains on her family.

**Myth 3: Because you and your new spouse love each other, you'll both automatically love your stepchildren, and they'll love you.** Fact: It takes time to develop loving, caring relationships. Your stepchildren can't help comparing you to their parents, and they need time to give up the notion that you must be exactly like their noncustodial parent. If you try to force your love on them, they're more likely to recoil than to embrace you.

Instead, approach your stepchildren the way you would approach a friend's children. You don't rush in to smother a friend's child with kisses and concern; you allow the child time to get used to you. Do the same with your stepchildren.

For instance, begin by sharing activities side by side, without expecting the children's love, gratitude, or even conversation. Start simply, spending only a short time together. Gradually your stepchildren will get used to spending more time with you. As they do, they'll become more comfortable sharing their fears, secrets, and giggles.

**Myth 4: By working hard to develop relationships, your stepfamily won't believe in a "Wicked Stepmother."** Fact: Unfortunately, the myth of the "Wicked Stepmother" is ingrained in our culture, which makes the stepmother's role painful at times. It's impossible to avoid some resentment on the part of the stepchildren. Many therapists find that stepmothers have a particularly hard time adjusting to the new family life, and link the problem to the many fairy tales about wicked stepmothers.

It's not easy for either stepparent. Eager to be a good stepparent, you may rush to assume all of the disciplinary responsibilities on your wedding day. However, stepchildren typically refuse to accept discipline from a stepparent until they have lived with that stepparent for 1½ to two years. It's better to wait to assume the disciplinary role until you have firmly established a relationship with the stepchildren.

In the meantime, you and your new spouse need to agree and support one another on family rules and on the consequences for breaking them. Although the stepparent shouldn't play the role of enforcer at first, the two of you can present a united front to the children and explain that they owe respect to both parents, and that you both agree on the rules you've established. Your children will feel more secure if they know they can't play one adult against the other.

Of course, there will be occasions when you are alone with the stepchildren and may need to discipline them. In those situations, follow the rules and consequences that you and your spouse have established. Make it clear to the children that you are acting as the authority figure in their parent's absence.

**Myth 5: If you read up on stepfamilies ahead of time, you won't feel guilty, jealous, or angry after you remarry.** Fact: All the preparation in the world can't stop your feelings. Feelings just come, and you can't prevent your reactions.

Reading and taking classes can help you understand what to expect, however. By preparing for your role as stepparent, you'll find some problems less surprising and perhaps easier to handle than they might have been otherwise.

Still, even the best-prepared stepparent probably will encounter some very trying times. Reading about problems in the abstract isn't the same as living with them. You may find that a stepparent support group gives you the comfort of knowing that others are experiencing similar difficulties. A therapist who is accustomed to stepfamilies may also help you sort out your turbulent feelings.

**Myth 6: Cutting off your son's contact with his noncustodial father will make him closer to his stepfather, and cutting off your daughter's contact with her noncustodial mother will make her closer to her stepmother.** Fact: This popular myth is based on the misconception that a clean break is best, and that time with the noncustodial parent takes too much time away from the developing relationship with the new stepparent. But the "clean break" fantasy is just that—a fantasy. Breaking off ties with a noncustodial parent only puts the child in more pain. In time, the child may come to resent you for causing so much pain.

Besides, no matter what you think of the ex-spouse, the child has learned to care about that parent and has a right to maintain the relationship. Keeping in touch with the noncustodial parent can only teach your child more about love and compassion. In time, what the child learns with that parent will generalize to the new stepparent and, eventually, to other people.

**Myth 7: If anything goes wrong, it's because you're in a stepfamily.** Fact: Many things go wrong in natural families, too. Parents are pressed for time and children may not appreciate parents' efforts. Even in intact families, children fight with each other and with their parents. The best all-American family may have a black sheep no one can explain.

In stepfamilies, conflict is even more likely. Stepfamilies have more people coming together with more expectations. In fact, for most couples, remarriage doesn't look anything like *The Brady Bunch.* Tempers flare, jealousy abounds, and feelings are easily hurt. So many people are adjusting to so many others that there are bound to be fireworks. If you can compare your stepfamily to a toddler in the midst of the "terrible twos" or to a teen caught up in the tumult of adolescence, you'll be able to consider the strife part of your new family's normal development.

In any event, don't give up. Even the most sullen and angry child does mature eventually. Keep the door of communication between you and your stepchildren open at least a crack. You may never be best buddies, but time heals many early wounds, and maturity can bring each of you a fresh perspective. Together you and your children have come a long way from the painful days of separation. And together you'll rebuild your family.

# Resources

## Support and Advocacy Groups: Children

Alateen
P.O. Box 862, Midtown Station
New York, NY 10018–0862
(800) 356-9996 or (212) 302-7240
Anonymous self-help groups for teenage children of alcoholics. National group can refer you to local support group that uses 12-step program. Literature available.

Big Brothers/Big Sisters of America
230 North 13th Street
Philadelphia, PA 19107
(215) 567-2748
Connects children of single-parent families with same-sex role models. Screens and trains role models before assigning them to children.

Boy Scouts of America
National Council
1325 Walnut Hill Lane
Irving, TX 75038-3096
(214) 580-2000
Offers general information and consulting services.

Girl Scouts of the U.S.A.
830 Third Avenue
New York, NY 10022
(212) 940-7500
Offers general information and consulting services.

## Support and Advocacy Groups: Adults

Al-Anon
P.O. Box 862, Midtown Station
New York, NY 10018–0862
(800) 356-9996 or (212) 302-7240
Anonymous self-help groups for family and friends of alcoholics. National group can refer you to local support group that uses 12-step program. Literature available.

American Association for Marriage and Family Therapy
924 West 9th Street
Upland, CA 91786
Professional association of therapists who have completed specialized training in marital and family therapy. Can refer you to therapists in your area.

Association for Children for Enforcement of Support
1018 Jefferson Avenue, No. 204
Toledo, OH 43624
Refers clients to local chapters of support groups, or, if no chapter exists, offers advice on how to start a group.

Fathers' Rights of America
P.O. Box 7596
Van Nuys, CA 91409
(818) 789-4435
Works on child custody, child support, divorce, and fathers' rights issues. Provides seminars and reference services.

Mothers Without Custody
P.O. Box 56762
Houston, TX 77256-6762
Offers local support groups for noncustodial mothers.